BOOK TWO

ALASKA BUSH COP

AND THE BEAT GOES ON

A.W. "ANDY" ANDERSON
ALASKA'S LONGEST SERVING POLICE CHIEF—RETIRED

PUBLICATION CONSULTANTS
We Believe In The Power Of Authors

PO Box 221974 Anchorage, Alaska 99522-1974
books@publicationconsultants.com—www.publicationconsultants.com

ISBN Number: 978-1-59433-959-2
eBook ISBN Number: 978-1-59433-960-8

Library of Congress Number: 2020912321

Manufactured in the United States of America

DEDICATION

Alaska Bush Cop, and the Beat Goes On,
is dedicated in loving memory of my wife Ann, and
to my daughter, Donica Mae and my Grandson, Westin Johnson.

Acknowledgement

I publicly acknowledge and thank Kathleen Gruber for all the time and effort she put into editing of Alaska Bush Cop.

TABLE OF CONTENTS

INTRODUCTION

This is the second of a series of four books I'm writing covering my nearly thirty-two years as a police chief for the city of Seldovia, Alaska. In August of 1979, when I started my police career, I was hired off the street by the city manager, who found himself in need of a police presence. I had no training and had really never anticipated being a police officer. Hiring a police officer off the street is not a common practice. When I took the position, I was told it would only be for a six-week period. The city manager later informed me, after doing background checks and some local checking on me, he felt I was the right man for the job. A position that was to be for only six weeks, turned into a thirty-two-year career, setting a record for the longest serving police chief for any city in Alaska history. I'm convinced the city manager stopped looking for anyone, once he pinned the badge on me.

I had moved to Seldovia, as a teenager, in May of 1964 and was well acquainted with almost everyone in town. I had worked in a number of different occupations, after arriving in Alaska, but this was by far the most challenging job I'd ever taken. In all my other positions I had a fairly good idea of what was expected of me but, not as a police officer. I contacted the Alaska State Troopers and the Homer police department's officers and dispatchers for advice and assistance. They took me under their wings and treated me as one of their own. Both departments nursed me along until I could stand on my own two feet. I would never advise anyone to enter into law enforcement without first obtaining some formal training, unless of course, you enjoy extreme challenges.

My first book in this series is entitled *Alaska Bush Cop, the Beginning*, and covers my police career for my first few years of service. During that timeframe, I was schooled in what an officer can and cannot do. Also, in the first book of the series, we travel through that critical learning curve where, due to a bad decision on my part, I was named in a lawsuit, along with the City of Seldovia. Due to my errors, which facilitated the lawsuit, the city decided I needed some formal training and arrangements were made for me to attend the Alaska State Trooper academy in Sitka, Alaska. The police academy was a real eye opener for me. I encourage you to read my first book, so you can witness the mistakes I made prior to going to the academy. By reading my first book you will also become acquainted with many of the people who took me under their wing and, when needed, gave me professional advice.

In this book I continue to cover my police career in the bush community of Seldovia, Alaska. The cases I talk about actually took place and are a matter of record in the Seldovia police department. I have my daily log books, and other reference materials, which I am using to research the facts of the cases I write about. Other than officers and close friends, the names I use will all be fictitious. This book is not written to embarrass or discredit anyone. It is my wish to educate and entertain the reader, and to be accurate as to how the cases and investigations took place. I will include cases we lost, or were unable to close, as well as those cases we did file criminal charges on.

For much of my career I found myself without a paid patrol officer. When the city could find funding for a position, I would be permitted to hire a patrol officer, and/or some clerical help, but, when the employee moved on to other employment opportunities, I would again find myself without an assistant due to budgetary restraints.

A very good friend of mine, John Gruber, was born and raised in Seldovia. When I was responding without backup, he was always ready, willing and able to accompany me on any call that was inherently dangerous. I cannot remember a time when he refused to assist me.

He is a man of integrity, who is very well known and very well liked in and around Seldovia. He has been blessed with good instincts and common sense. I felt honored to have him covering my back on the many different responses over my career and he never disappointed me on any of these calls. Any actions taken by Officer Gruber were needed and he always made good decisions. Many times, when we were advertising for an officer, I would encourage John to apply for the permanent position, but he said he didn't want to take it on full-time, however he said he would assist me when he was needed. He also assisted some of my patrol officers throughout the years, but most of his responses were with me.

POLICING A SMALL COMMUNITY

Having been a police officer in a small community for so many years, I feel I have a pretty good idea of what it takes to survive in a law enforcement position in a small area. When I say survive, I'm referring to being able to put up with the petty politics, which are vicious at times, the constant critiquing by local citizens, while making yourself available twenty four hours a day, seven days a week, and being required to work under so many different city managers. I personally worked under twenty-three different city managers, in my nearly thirty-two years of service. Each of the city managers had a different management style and, at times, I would not agree with the manager's philosophy. However, I had to find a middle ground or seek employment elsewhere. You have to be able to get along with nearly everyone, to survive as a cop in a small area. I must admit, at times it was very difficult to not just walk away without looking back.

You also have to be able to bring criminal charges, or write citations, when dealing with acquaintances, friends or family, who have violated the law. This is probably the most stressful of all the cases you will become involved in as a small-town cop. Most police officers, in a small community, only last for two to three years, if that, due to the different stresses of the job. In a lot of ways, a person who does police a small community, is under many stresses that officers from larger police departments rarely experience. 99% of the time, a small-town police officer is dealing with people with whom he/she is acquainted, or people they have a close relationship with. On these occasions it would be very easy to look the other way and give them a pass, but if you are honest in your dealings, you cannot turn your head. If you look the other way one time, you will have to continue turning your head for the rest of your career. Honesty and fairness are everything in a small community. People are watching how you do the job and you are building a reputation within the community. That reputation can be either good or bad. Benjamin Franklin once said, "It takes many good deeds to build a good reputation, but it only takes one bad one to lose it." You don't want to be caught in the trap of giving a buddy, or relative, a break due to your relationship. If you do it once, you must give breaks to everyone all the time, regardless of who they are.

What helped me personally, to continue in the police effort for nearly thirty-two years in our small community was, first, and most importantly, my family. I had worked away from home for so many years before taking the badge, I never wanted to have to leave home for employment again. In my case, the daily support from my loved ones was the catalyst that held it all together. I certainly couldn't have continued, at times, without the support my wife, Ann, and daughter, Donica. They also encouraged me to quit my job, on more than one occasion, due to the politics, the stresses of the job and the different city managers who I didn't see eye to eye with. But these things are inevitable in a small community. How you deal with stress, will determine how long you last as a police officer. That applies to officers who work in larger communities, as well as those who work in smaller communities.

Being up front and honest, regardless of who you are dealing with, is vitally important. You must treat everyone the same. On my first day in office I decided I would live by the motto of *"I'll treat a drunk like a preacher and treat a preacher like a drunk."* In other words, treat everyone equal, regardless of who they may be. Most times the person violating the law, regardless of who it was, have already made my decisions for me, before I ever reach the scene. I had the Municipal Code, the State Statutes and the Federal Statutes as my guidelines and, in most cases, the actions taken by the suspect has already determined what my actions would be. I really didn't have a lot of decisions to make many times when I arrived on scene. I only had to do what was mandated by City, State or Federal law. I had a lot of discretion when writing citations, but not when I dealt with misdemeanors or felonies.

As a child I was taught to show everyone respect even if you didn't respect them. Being respectful does not mandate that you be friends, or even like someone. If you treat people with respect, most times, they will show you respect in return. I found it invaluable throughout my career. But then there are those who, I'm convinced, don't know the definition of the word respect.

You also must keep yourself available to the public seven days a week, twenty-four hours a day, to survive in a small community. You must resign yourself to the fact that, unless you leave town, you will not have any real time off. I've had many people come to my home for assistance, regardless of the time of day or night, and regardless of whether on a holiday or on a weekend. I've had victims bleeding all over the floor in my foyer. I've had numerous people come to my home seeking protection, after being in an altercation. The public expects you to protect them and that is your primary duty as a police officer. When you take the oath of office, you swore to protect and serve the public, and I took my oath seriously. I certainly had no idea my family would be so impacted by my job, or I might have had second thoughts about taking the position.

Honesty, being respectful and being available, are the three most important factors, when policing a small community. These traits are vitally important in a small department. In the less populated areas, you are well known by most everyone, and the public is watching to see how you do the job. If you tell someone you are going to do something, you should never fail to carry through, and do as you had promised. You are always trying to build the public's trust and, if you're successful, you'll find your job becomes easier, and you'll have considerably more assistance from the public, when you need it.

This is my philosophy for policing a small community. I attribute this philosophy to my longevity. As a police officer, people expect considerably more of you, than when they were just an acquaintance.

With that said, let's continue exploring more of the cases and investigations which took place in, and around, my hometown of Seldovia, Alaska.

DISORDERLY CONDUCT

On July 7, 1987, just after midnight, Officer John Gruber received a call from his sister, who was bartending at the Seldovia Lodge. She reported an adult male, who we will call Tommy, was intoxicated and causing trouble in the bar and when she asked him to leave, he refused to do so.

Officer Gruber called Officer Jerry Lewis, and told him of the report. Lewis told Officer Gruber he would respond and pick him up in his patrol vehicle. As Lewis was responding to pick up Officer Gruber, he observed Tommy walking down Seldovia Street. The officer contacted Tommy, to ascertain his degree of intoxication, and he asked him what was going on. Tommy immediately started cursing the officer and then he threatened to kill him. Officer Gruber lived just up the hill from where Officer Lewis had contacted Tommy and, after observing the two, he hurried down to their location. When he arrived on scene, Tommy cursed him and threatened to kill him, as well. Tommy then made an aggressive gesture, walking toward the officer with both fists clenched, and his arms held in a fighting stance. Officer Gruber reacted immediately, hitting Tommy twice in the face. Tommy went down hard. Officer Lewis rolled Tommy onto his stomach, and placed him in handcuffs, while advising him he was under arrest for disorderly conduct.

I had been monitoring the call on the radio, and the response by Officer Lewis. I had gotten out of bed, dressed and responded, arriving on scene just as Officer Lewis was placing Tommy in handcuffs. Tommy was cursing both officers and was very unruly. He was yelling he had been assaulted by Officer Gruber. Officer Lewis told me Tommy had approached Officer Gruber in a fighting stance, and Officer Gruber was only defending himself. Tommy was transported to the Seldovia Police Department, booked, photographed and placed in the jail cell. When his Miranda warning was read to him, Tommy refused to sign it and requested an attorney.

He was highly intoxicated and was belligerent during the booking process. He kept making verbal threats throughout the entire process. The threats were all recorded on a voice recorder which Officer Lewis had activated just prior to his contact with the subject. The Seldovia police officers had repeatedly dealt with Tommy, so we had a very good idea of what to expect from him. He was always verbally abusive, when he was intoxicated, and he was often physically aggressive, as well. He had been arrested on numerous occasions, on domestic violence assaults and for fighting in the bars. He wasn't driving at the time, due to the loss of his license, stemming from a previous DWI. Alcohol was very prevalent in Tommy's life.

The magistrate in Homer was called and bail was set at $500 cash. Tommy couldn't make bail, so a guard was hired and, Tommy spent the night in the cell. At approximately 0950 hours, the following morning, he was released on his own recognizance, after he had sobered up somewhat, and after signing a promise to appear for arraignment on charges of disorderly conduct. The arraignment was set for July 12, 1987 at 1330 hours, in Homer court. The release form also mandated that he not consume any alcoholic beverages or enter any establishment whose main purpose was the sale of alcohol.

Tommy did appear for his arraignment in the Homer court, and he pled no contest. He was found guilty of disorderly conduct. He was fined $100 and was placed on probation for two years. With his criminal record, we in the Police Department were disappointed, in that he didn't receive some jail time, but it was only a class "B" misdemeanor. We did our job and we would continue to keep these type people under control as best we could. (Case Closed by Arrest)

NOTE: *Tommy was one of our repeat offenders (a frequent flyer) who, when intoxicated, had no respect for anyone or anything, including the law. He was, what we referred to in the police department, as job security. We would always have work as long as people like Tommy existed in our society. I guess we should have been more beholding to them, but that wasn't going to happen. I'm afraid most all communities have Tommy's in their mists. This is a reason a police presence is so important. You never know when the Tommy's of our world will show out and have to be dealt with. As you read about the following cases, you will see Tommy's name come up again and again.*

Driving While Intoxicated (DWI), Refuse Breath Test

On July 24, 1987, at approximately 2040 hours, while on patrol, I observed a Subaru station wagon driving approximately forty mile per hour in a twenty-five mile per hour zone on Winifred Avenue at Anderson Way. The vehicle was traveling in a southerly direction and was observed to swerve into the left lane on two occasions. I activated my overhead lights, and when the operator saw my lights, he pulled into a parking area at 271 English Drive. The driver, who we'll call Howard, immediately exited his vehicle and started toward my patrol vehicle. I yelled for him to stop and I approached him. He handed me his driver's license and said, "Here, see I've got a driver's license." I took the license and I observed a smell of alcohol on his breath and I noticed his cheeks were flushed and his eyes were bloodshot. His voice was also somewhat slurred.

As I was talking to him, his girlfriend, who we'll call Alice, exited the vehicle and she grabbed the license out of my hand and put it in her pocket. She cursed me and said I was just out to get her boyfriend. Since she was looking for an argument, I ignored her, and continued to deal with the driver. I asked him to perform a series of field sobriety tests. The first test I requested of him was to recite the American alphabet from the letter "A" to the letter "Z" without singing it. He told me he couldn't recite the alphabet backwards and I told him that wasn't what I was asking of him. I again ask him to recite the alphabet from the letter

"A" to the letter "Z" and he attempted it but left out some letters. Alice was trying to help him and I told her if she didn't stop interfering, she would be arrested. She cursed me again and then walked over by the Subaru. Howard then attempted the alphabet again but stopped before reaching the end. He attempted it on two more occasions and failed both times. I then ask that he count backwards from ninety-seven to seventy-six and he attempted this twice and on the last occasion he kept counting, stopping at sixty-five instead of seventy-six. I then showed him the heel to toe test and asked him to take six steps forward then to turn around and take five steps back, touching the toes of his foot with the heel of his other foot on each step. He was unable to correctly complete this test, as well. He failed to touch the heel to the toes on the opposite foot and he took too many steps in both directions. On three occasions he had to step to the side to keep from falling. I then asked that he blow on the portable breath test instrument and he refused, stating he would never blow on one of those things. I told him he would be cited and it would cost him $50 if he refused. He still refused to blow. I informed him he was under arrest for driving while intoxicated and I placed him in handcuffs and put him in the back seat of the patrol vehicle. Alice had been cursing me throughout most of the testing and kept repeating I was just out to get them. I told her to give me Howard's driver's license and surprisingly, without an argument, she handed it to me. She then cursed me again and started to enter the driver's side of the Subaru. I told her if she got under the wheel of the vehicle, I would be arresting her for driving while intoxicated, as well. That initiated another stream of profanities, which would make a logger blush, but she didn't get into the vehicle. I walked over to the car and took the key and locked the vehicle. It was in a parking lot so it wasn't a traffic hazard and I could leave it where it was parked.

I transported Howard to the police department and again put him through the verbal part of the field sobriety tests. He attempted them but failed both the alphabet and the counting and he refused any further tests.

After observing him with nothing in his mouth for a period of twenty-five minutes, I requested he blow on the Intoximeter but he refused to give a breath sample. I read the implied consent form to him, which specifically told him he would be charged with an additional crime, a class A misdemeanor, if he refused to submit to a breath sample, but he still refused. I rolled his fingerprints and took his mug shots and then called the magistrate on call for the Homer court. Bail was set at $500 cash and Alice brought a check for him to sign. She then went to the bar and got the cash to bail him out. He signed a promise to appear on charges of driving while intoxicated and failure to submit to a breath test. I wrote him a citation for failing to provide a portable breath test and he was released on his on $500.00 bail.

At arraignment Howard pled not guilty and a trial date was set. Prior to the trial taking place, a plea bargain was reached between his attorney and the district attorney. At this point he pled guilty to driving while intoxicated and refusing a breath test was dismissed. Howard lost his license for ninety days and he was fined $500 with $250 suspended. He was given thirty days in jail with all but seventy-two hours suspended and was ordered to undertake alcohol screening at South Kachemak Inc. Alcoholism Program (SKIAP). He was placed on probation for two years with orders not to violate any laws during the probationary period.

It takes a lot of time to ready a case for prosecution and the paperwork is astronomical. I say this to educate those who read my writings and have a predisposed idea that the officers of a police department in a small community do nothing but drive around. I've actually been told that a police position in a small city has to be a walk in the park. Having served for nearly thirty-two years, I'm well aware of what the job consists of and it isn't what most people think. I enjoyed the job most of the time, when I could actually assist people and make their lives better, but I didn't really get a thrill out of always having to tell people what they were doing wrong. A police officer is sworn to serve and to keep the citizens safe and, if we take our oaths seriously, we will be busy enforcing the rules and don't have a lot of "me" time. I know this is where my family suffered but, on the other side of the coin, I was able to stay home and not have to leave town to make a living. Sometimes we have to sacrifice to make other things we want a reality. I am not complaining, only trying to educate those who really feel the job is a walk in the park. It is somewhat demanding with calls coming in all times of the day and night and all the investigations and cases which have to be filed. There is an old saying in the police world which is, *"If it's not written down, it didn't happen."* so we keep impeccable records of every action we take. We also must finalize the necessary paperwork which is mandated for cases filed in a court of law which are sent to the district attorney's office. On the bright side, my typing skills increased. (Case Closed by Arrest)

Driving While Intoxicated and Felony Evading

On August 9,1987, at approximately 0120 hours, Officer Lewis observed a blue Chevrolet van traveling westbound on Main Street without any lights on. The officer pulled in behind the van and activated his overhead lights. The van immediately picked up speed and headed north on Seldovia Street. The van then ran the stop sign at the Seldovia Street and Alder Street intersection and continued in a northerly direction onto Anderson Way then onto Jakolof Bay Road. Officer Lewis called me on the radio and told me he had a vehicle failing to stop for him and they were headed out the Jakolof Bay Road. I quickly geared up and ran to my patrol vehicle and joined the pursuit.

When we were nearing two- and one-half mile, Jakolof Bay Road, the driver of the van locked up the breaks and came to a sliding stop. When Officer Lewis and I approached the vehicle, we observed only a female driver in the vehicle. She was asked to produce an operator's license and her vehicle registration. She produced both but was having some difficulty finding the operator license. Her speech was slurred and she smelled of alcohol. I asked her why she didn't stop when she saw the police behind her and she said she thought we were after someone else and she didn't know we wanted her to stop. She appeared to be having problems focusing. I ask her how much she'd had to drink and she told me two beers. Her eyes were bloodshot and her face appeared flushed.

After she did produce the operator license and the registration to the vehicle, she was asked to step out of the van. She was observed to be very unsteady and she was holding onto the door of the vehicle to maintain her balance. When I asked her where she was headed, she told me she was going out the road but she didn't' have a specific destination she would divulge. It was approaching 0200 hours and the driver lived in town so it was unclear what her destination was. I asked her to recite the American alphabet from the letter "A" to the letter "Z" and she attempted it on two occasions but could not complete it either time. I then requested she count backwards from eighty-seven to fifth four and she was unable to complete this test as well, leaving some numbers out. She was then asked to do a balance test where she was directed to stand with both feet together, to lean her head back and look at the sky, then to close her eyes until I counted to thirty. She attempted this test and nearly fell down so we stopped the test and didn't repeat it. She was then asked to do the heel to toe test and I showed her what was expected of her. I asked that she take five steps forward, turn around then take six steps back. When she attempted this test, she failed to ever touch her heel to her toe, she just walked up a few steps, turned around and walked back. I informed her she was under arrest for driving while intoxicated and I handcuffed her and placed her in my vehicle in the front passenger seat. I put her seat belt on her and then transported her to the police department. Officer Lewis pulled her van off the road and locked it then joined us at the police department.

Upon reaching the police department I took the handcuffs off and had her have a seat facing my desk. I filled out the necessary paperwork and read her the implied consent form. After having observed her for thirty minutes, wherein I could attest to the fact that she had put nothing in her mouth, I asked that she provide a sample of her breath. She blew on the Intoximeter which resulted in a reading of .250 blood alcohol. Following the breath test and, after being photographed and fingerprinted, she was placed in a jail cell for the night. A female guard was called and came in to jail guard.

At approximately 1000 hours, after signing a promise to appear for her court arraignment on charges of driving while intoxicated and failure to stop at the direction of a police officer, she was released on her own recognizance.

At her arraignment the defendant pled no contest to both charges and, on the driving while intoxicated, she was sentenced to thirty days in jail with all but seventy two hours suspended, she was given a fine of $500 with $250 suspended, her operator's license was revoked for ninety days and was ordered to undertake alcohol screening at SKIAP . She was placed on probation for one year. On the charge of failure to stop at the direction of a police officer she was fined $500 with $400 suspended and was placed on probation for one year, which ran concurrent with the driving while intoxicated sentence. (Case Closed by Arrest)

NOTE: *The Seldovia police department had a zero-tolerance policy when it came to driving while intoxicated. We let it be known in the community we would arrest anyone, regardless of who you were, if you drove while you were intoxicated. Many people felt they could evade being caught, I guess, because we continued to have people drive while they were impaired. We even told the bars we would give the people a ride home if they could not find another ride. This also failed to be a deterrent. We continued our efforts and they continued to drive drunk so we continued to enforce the law. They did evade us, I'm sure, on many occasions but the odds were, they would get caught sometime if they continued to drive when they were drinking. Each time they got caught the fines, the jail time and the length of time they lost their privilege to drive, got longer and longer and even that didn't deter some of them. It seemed strange to me that many of those we did arrest, for DWI more than once, always seemed to blame the officer for their actions. I guess they have to blame someone when they refuse to take responsibility for their own actions. Oh well!*

FUGITIVE FROM JUSTICE

On August 11, 1987, at approximately 1030 hours, I received a call from the Alaska State Troopers in Anchorage asking me if I would check with the John Cabot cannery to see if they had a man working there who was a fugitive from justice. They gave me the suspect's name and told me he was wanted out of Oklahoma on two counts of murder, two counts of leaving the scene of an injury accident and three counts of assault with a deadly weapon. The trooper told me the young man and his girlfriend had broken up and he was upset and was stalking her. When he saw her with another man, leaving a drive-in movie, he forced their vehicle into the path of another vehicle with his pickup truck, and caused a head on collision. The collision killed two of the occupants, one being his ex-girlfriend, and injured three other occupants. After I finished talking with the Alaska State Troopers, I called the cannery superintendent and gave him the fugitive's name and asked if the man was working at the cannery. I was told he would have to check his employment roster. In a short time, the superintendent called me back and said the man I was looking for was working at the cannery and he said, he would be at the cannery, and not at the bunkhouse, because they were processing today.

After I was sure the man was working at the cannery, I called Officer Lewis and told him we had a fugitive from justice that we needed to pick up. Officer Lewis told me he would gear up and come right down. After Officer Lewis arrived, we took my patrol vehicle and drove to the John Cabot cannery. We entered the Office and

23

contacted the superintendent, who immediately took us to the break room and pointed out the fugitive. The suspect was setting alone at a table. I drew my weapon and approached the man. Holding the man at gunpoint, I told him he was under arrest for the murder of two people and I ordered him to stand up and put his hands on the wall. He did as he was directed and I patted him down for weapons. Finding no weapons, I handcuffed the man behind his back and took him into custody. He was then thoroughly searched, but no weapons were found. We walked the man into the office area and again contacted the superintendent and told him we would be taking the man out of Seldovia. The superintendent asked him if he had any personal belongings and he stated he only had what he was wearing. We then left the cannery and took the suspect to the police department where he was booked and locked in a jail cell.

(*When arresting the man, I brandished my weapon because I didn't know him and I wanted him to know he had nowhere to go. I didn't know if he was armed or not but, he was a fugitive, so I took no chances.*)

I called the Alaska State Troopers in Anchorage and told them the man was in custody and we would be transporting him to Homer where I would be turning him over to AST at the Homer post. They thanked us for our assistance and I made arrangements for the flight to Homer. I called Trooper Steve Smith and he agreed to meet us and take the fugitive off my hands at the Homer airport.

At 1430 hours I transported the fugitive to the Seldovia airport and we took a Cook Inlet Aviation aircraft to Homer. Trooper Smith met us at Cook Inlet aviation and took custody of the fugitive and transported him to the Homer jail. After delivering the prisoner to trooper Smith, I returned to Seldovia.

After I returned to my office, the superintendent of the cannery brought me a number of items he said belonged to the fugitive. These included a sleeping bag, clothes and some toiletries. I packaged the items up and then called the Homer Jail and inquired what the fugitive wanted done with the items he'd left behind. The jailer inquired of him and told me he requested we mail them to his grandmother and he supplied an address. The next day I mailed the package to the address he gave us. (Case Closed by Arrest)

NOTE: *The young man I arrested was twenty-one years of age and was a fugitive from justice on five felony charges and would most probably spend the next fifty plus years behind bars. This was all because he let his emotions dictate his actions. I found him to be nothing more than a frightened kid. It was sad and, I'm sure, heartbreaking for his loved ones. I've seen it over and over again, when we had to arrest people who commit criminal acts, simply because they are unhappy with something that happened or they want to get revenge against someone. What they do in one split second, negatively affects their entire future. I would hope people would think of the consequences for their actions before they just react and let their emotions guide them. Most times it's because they want to even a score or they are upset with someone. In this instance we have another life ruined by a split-second reaction on his part.*

BURGLARY OF THE LOCAL MARKET

On October 18, 1987, at approximately 2340 hours, I received a call from Marietta Beymer, manager of the Seldovia Market, stating she had just received an alarm, indicating someone had forced entry into the store. Ms. Beymer was the manager of the business and lived in one of the apartments located above the store. The burglar alarm was piped into her apartment.

As soon as I received the report, I called Officer Lewis on the police radio and told him about the call. I told him to meet me at the store and for him to take the back and I'd take the front. When Ms. Beymer had called, I told her to meet me at the front of the store so I could enter from that location. I further instructed her not to enter until I and Officer Lewis arrived.

When I arrived Officer Lewis and Ms. Beymer were already waiting outside the store. I told Officer Lewis to check the rear of the store and I'd check the front. Ms. Beymer was told to wait by the police vehicle until we checked to see it there was a forced entry. Upon checking the rear of the store, Officer Lewis called on the radio and told me he'd located a forced entry, with tool marks, on the rear entry door. Ms. Beymer unlocked the front door and I called Officer Lewis on the radio and told him I was entering the front and for him to come in through the rear of the store. Upon entry Officer Lewis and I started a grid search. A couple minutes had passed when I heard Officer Lewis directing someone to drop the crowbar and lay face down on the floor. I hurried to Officer Lewis' location to find him with his weapon drawn and holding it on a man dressed in dark clothing. The man was lying on the floor, with his arms stretched out in front of him. I observed a crowbar lying by the man's side and I kicked it away from him and, while Officer Lewis held the man at gunpoint, I placed the him in handcuffs.

In my search of the store I had observed a black garbage bag to be lying in one of the isles and it appeared to have some items inside it. I didn't stop and check it at that time but, with the man now in custody, I retrieved the bag and found some food items inside. The man said he'd broken in because he was hungry and needed food. The man was also packing a plastic garbage bag with food items in it, as well.

While I transported the prisoner to the police department, Officer Lewis assisted Ms. Beymer in securing the back door. Officer Lewis took photographs of the tool marks and the door being ajar prior to securing it.

Upon reaching the police department, the suspect was given his Miranda warning and signed his waiver of rights form and agreed to talk to me. He said he had broken into the store because he didn't have any food and hadn't eaten for a couple days. When asked if he had ever done anything like this before, he told me he had broken into another store in Kenai and had been caught there, too. He said he was on probation and would probably go to jail for a long time. I told him he might want to pursue a different occupation as he wasn't very good at burglary.

An inventory was taken of the bag he had with him, and most of the items were edible. They consisted of the following: two, one-pound packages of bacon, two cartons of Marlboro cigarettes, two, one-pound packages of hot link sausages, two, one-pound tubs of Gold-n-Soft margarine and the garbage bag. The other garbage bag containing food stuffs was not taken as evidence.

The suspect was booked and placed in a cell. I did the necessary paperwork so he could be arraigned on felony charges of burglary not in a dwelling; and the following morning, I transported him to Homer, where he was incarcerated awaiting arraignment. At his arraignment he was given a high bail, which he could not make, and he remained in jail pending a bail review hearing. He was given a public defender and later pled no contest to the charges. He was found guilty and sentenced to twenty-four months in jail with twenty-two months suspended, leaving sixty days to serve. He was given five years' probation and he was fined $1000.00 with $500.00 suspended. (Case Closed by Arrest)

NOTE: *The alarm system in the store had been installed the month prior to this burglary and the owners felt they had made a great investment, after it was instrumental in catching the burglar in the act. The alarm was later upgraded to call the police department's phone with a recorded message indicating whether it was a burglary or there was a fire. At times the alarm would be activated but no entry could be found, but we were thankful it did work on that one occasion. I'm sure, when the word got around town about the alarm being the reason the man was caught, it deterred other would-be burglars.*

DOMESTIC VIOLENCE AND ASSAULT WITH A DEADLY WEAPON

On December 25, 1987, Christmas Day, at approximately 2140 hours, I received a call from a man reporting the police were needed at his residence as soon as possible. He reported his step-daughter had tried to stab her mother. Officer Lewis was called and told of the report and he responded immediately. I was at home and had to get geared up and then I responded. When Officer Lewis arrived on scene, he contacted the complainant and asked what was going on. The complainant told him he wanted to wait for me to arrive, because I was acquainted with the problem and had been involved previously in a matter involving his step-daughter. He told Officer Lewis he had taken a knife away from his step-daughter after she had tried to stab her mother. Officer Lewis observed blood on the complainant's hand and ask if he needed medical attention. He said he did not and no one in the residence was injured to the point of needing medical assistance.

I arrived on scene and Officer Lewis brought me up to speed on what had occurred. We entered the residence and I observed the mother and the step-daughter sitting in the living room. I also observed a small amount of blood on the step-daughter's right hand. I ask her if she needed medical attention and she said she did not. After hearing the story from both the step-daughter and the parents I told the step-daughter to get her things together because she was coming with me.

The step-daughter had been taken out of the home by the Division of Family and Youth Services (DFYS) the previous year, due to allegations she had made concerning her step-father but they had allowed her to come home for a Christmas visit. The girl had gotten into an argument with her mother, after they had arrived home from the bar and found her to have a boy in her bedroom. The boy was kicked out and the step-daughter and her mother got into a verbal altercation which turned physical. The daughter told the police she grabbed a knife after her mother started hitting her and she had to defend herself. She never stabbed her mother because her step-father took the knife away from her. She grabbed another knife from the drawer, a steak knife, and the step-father again took it away from her. In the tussle both the step-daughter and the step-father sustained small cuts on their hands. Nothing observed by the officer would require any medical assistance.

I took the step-daughter to the Seldovia Police Department and called Ron Harper, of DFYS. Arrangements were made for a safe home in Seldovia for the night and the girl would be sent to Homer when it was daylight and the airplanes could fly. She had already been scheduled for a flight at 1045 hours the next morning, prior to the altercation with her parents.

I read the girl her Miranda warning and she signed her waiver of rights form and agreed to talk to me. She said her parents had gone out to the bars and she was at home, taking care of her little brother. She said a male friend had come by to visit and they had gone to her bedroom to talk so her little brother would not hear what was said. She said she wasn't doing anything wrong but when the parents came home, her little brother told them she had a boy in her bedroom. They became angry and kicked the boy out and she said her mother started hitting her. She said she grabbed a knife to defend herself. She told me both her mother and her step-father were hitting her and the only way to make them stop was by grabbing a knife. She said she didn't do anything wrong with the boy and they had no reason to get angry.

Ron Harper of DFYS called back and told me to take the girl to the safe home he'd located. I told him I would be filling a report with juvenile intake reference assault with a deadly weapon charge and he agreed that the juvenile intake system should be brought into the matter.

I delivered the girl to the safe home and told her I'd be picking her up in the morning to take her to the airport for her flight back to Homer. I instructed her to be ready around 1000 hours and we'd stay with the schedule she had already made with the airlines.

After delivering the girl to the safe home, I returned to the residence of her mother and step-father and interviewed each of them separately. Both were also given their Miranda warning and both signed a waiver of rights form and agreed to talk to me.

Both the mother and the step-father were interviewed separately and both told the same story. They had arrived home and their son told them their daughter had a boy in her bedroom, a rule she had broken on more than one occasion. They always forbid any boys to be in their daughter's bedroom. Both also stated the step-father had not done anything more than take the two knives away from the step-daughter and that he never hit her at any time. She and her mother had come to blows after the daughter had hit her mother first. They were both disappointed and said everything had been going so well during the daughter's visit then it seemed to all fall apart.

I told the parents I would be filing a report with the juvenile intake system and they would most probably have to talk with Eric Weatherby. They said they would do whatever they were required to do.

I left their residence, following the interviews, and responded to the police department where I started the case for filing with the juvenile intake system. The paperwork was filed but I do not know what the end result was. I often did not find out what the dispositions were in Juvenile cases.

I had been involved with the family in a previous matter when the step-daughter had accused the step-father of two counts of sexual assault and later, after her interviews were inconsistent on important issues, she had recanted and admitted no sexual assault had occurred. It would be an understatement to say the relationship with her step-father was strained. Her credibility also had to be taken into consideration in any future cases she became involved in. (Case Closed by Referral to Juvenile Intake)

1987 ANNUAL ACTIVITIES

The police department was again busy during the 1987 year. We had a person trying to evade police, another person interfered with an arrest, we had one search & rescue, one minor in possession of alcohol, three registration violations, two disorderly conduct situations, six motor vehicle accidents, one murder in the second degree, one suspicious circumstance, six driving while intoxicated investigations, one drowning, four assaults, one warrant arrest, eight thefts reports investigated, two criminal trespass reports, one sexual assault of a minor, two driving while license revoked, one fugitive from justice arrest, one stop sign citation written, one burglary, one person driving with no driver's license, one report of person passing a school bus while the lights were illuminated, and one person refused a breath test. These were the case files generated but do not include all the incidents that took place. We average between five hundred and eight hundred incidents per year, depending on the year. Everything is documented in a police department. There is an old saying that "If it isn't written down, it didn't happen" so, we had to keep impeccable records. This equates to a lot of hours on the typewriter. We had no computers during this era and it took a lot longer to type the incidents and cases.

ASSAULT WITH A DEADLY WEAPON AND WEAPONS MISCONDUCT 2ND DEGREE

On May 30, 1988, at approximately 0410 hours, I received a call from a distraught man telling me he had nearly been shot and needed the police. He said his roommate had come home intoxicated and had drawn two pistols on him and had threatened to kill him. He said he had pointed both pistols at him and he thought he was going to die. He said he ran out of the apartment expecting anytime to hear a gunshot. I told the man to walk to the police department and we'd meet him at that location.

I called Officer Lewis and told him about the report. Officer Lewis said he'd meet me at the police department. I dressed quickly, geared up and responded to the police department. The victim was already there and shortly thereafter Officer Lewis arrived.

In talking to the victim at the police department, I was told his roommate came home intoxicated and had awakened him. Being upset, the victim said he grabbed a filet knife and was rubbing it back and forth on the wall as if he was sharpening it, in hopes this would deter his roommate so he would leave him alone. He said he heard two clicks and looked up, seeing two pistols pointed at his head. He described the two pistols as one being a Sterling .22 automatic pistol and the other a 10 MM Colt, automatic pistol. He said the suspect pointed both of the weapons at his head and told him he should just shoot him right now. Then he told him to get out or he'd shoot him and the victim said he ran out the door. He said he didn't even have time to put his shoes on. It was then I noticed he was barefoot. I told the victim to stay at the police department and we would be back to talk more with him.

Officer Lewis and I took my vehicle and drove to the apartment building. We proceeded up the steps and located apartment number seven. I knocked on the door and announced we were the police and for the suspect to open the door. After getting no response I again knocked on the door, harder this time, and I yelled out that it was the police and for him to open the door. Still there was no response so I again knocked loudly on the door and again announced it was the police and we needed to talk to him. On this occasion the suspect told us to come on in. I again told him to open the door and he opened it approximately one foot and said for us to come on in. From where I was standing, I could not see the suspect but Officer Lewis could see his right hand and yelled for him to drop the pistol. I pushed the door open with my foot where I could see him and, in his right hand he was holding the 10 MM Colt automatic pistol, the victim told us about. I also observed the weapon to be in full cocked position. Officer Lewis again ordered him to drop the weapon. Both Officer Lewis and I had our weapons drawn and were now aiming them center mass at the suspect. His weapon was being held with it pointing at the ceiling. The man was not following any of our commands and we had no way of knowing what he would do next. The suspect stepped to his left and Officer Lewis dove at him. Upon seeing Officer Lewis move, I grabbed the suspect's arm which was holding the weapon. We were able to subdue him before he could respond. I disarmed him and placed him in handcuffs while Officer Lewis held him down. In checking the weapon, I found the 10 MM Colt to have the safety on but when I cleared it, I found a round to be in the chamber and 6 more rounds in the magazine. All the rounds were Hornady hollow points. What was frightening was that neither Officer Lewis or I had time to holster our weapons before taking the suspect down and disarming him. Luckily, neither Officer Lewis's nor my weapon accidentally discharged.

After the suspect was in handcuffs, I looked around the apartment and I observed the .22 caliber automatic pistol, the victim had described, lying on the kitchen counter. I found the filet knife in the hallway on the floor, between the bedroom and the living room. I cleared the Sterling .22 caliber automatic pistol and found it was loaded with one in the chamber and four more in the magazine. All the bullets were long rifle hollow points. All three weapons were taken as evidence.

The apartment was secured and the suspect was transported to the police department where the victim was still waiting. The suspect was so intoxicated, I decided to just do the booking procedure and then interview him the next morning, when he'd had some time to sober up.

I told the victim to go on home and get some rest and I'd talk to him later in the day. He asked if he could get a ride because his feet were hurting since he'd been walking around barefoot. Officer Lewis said he'd give him a ride home.

I called a jail guard and had him come in to guard the prisoner. I booked the suspect and fingerprinted him while waiting on the jail guard. I took the photographs needed then put the suspect in the jail cell.

Later that morning, at approximately 1100 hours, I brought the suspect into the office and read him his Miranda warning. He refused to sign the waiver of rights form and refused to be interviewed. He was again locked in the jail cell.

I called the district attorney and informed him what had taken place and I told him I wanted to charge three felony assaults, one on the victim and two on Officer Lewis and myself. I also told him I wanted to charge him with felony weapons misconduct in the second degree. The district attorney instructed me to charge three charges of assault in the fourth degree and one weapon's misconduct in the third degree, all misdemeanors instead of felonies. I argued my point to the district attorney but he insisted on misdemeanor charges instead of felonies.

I've found time and time again the charges we brought against suspects were most often reduced by the district attorney's office, if not dismissed, and I've always felt it was due to our geographical location. The costs are greater to prosecute a case in Seldovia than in Homer, Kenai, Soldotna, or Seward. For that reason, we seemed to always get our charges reduced, or have them dismissed all together. This was just another one of those instances that occurred throughout my career. If we charge a felony the DA has to either convene a grand jury or have a preliminary hearing within a short amount of time. This could very well be another reason they try to dismiss or lesson the charges on suspects charged in Seldovia. It is certainly not fair to the victims of the crimes as well as the officers who put their life on the line and spend the time and effort to hold suspects accountable under the law.

I did charge the four misdemeanors and I transported the suspect to the Homer Jail where he awaited his arraignment. He pled not guilty at arraignment and a $5000 cash only bail was ordered by the judge. He was unable to make bail and spent quite a long period of time behind bars before his calendar call. NOTE: *A calendar call is when the suspect has an opportunity to change his plea and it is also the time when the court sets the date and time of trial.*

The suspects attorney, a public defender, and the district attorney had discussed the charges against the suspect and a plea agreement was reached. They agreed, if the suspect would plead guilty to 1 assault and the weapons misconduct charge, the other two assaults would be dropped. Even though the felony charges that I wanted to charge were reduced to misdemeanors, even two of them were dismissed.

The judge sentenced the suspect to two years in jail with all but sixty days suspended, ordering the suspect serve the sixty days, but he was given credit for the time he had already served. He only spent a couple additional weeks in jail following the sentencing. He was also fined $500 with $250 suspended, ordered to undergo alcohol screening and he was placed on probation for two years

A number of things could have gone wrong so easily in this case. The victim could have gotten shot or killed, the suspect could have shot at Officer Lewis or myself and we could have been injured or killed and the situation may have resulted in our shooting the suspect. With the exception of the charges, which were brought by the district attorney, everything went as well as it could go. No one was injured or killed and the matter was brought to a conclusion through the courts.

Often, we had to put ourselves in harm's way to protect the public, but that comes with the job description. However, we felt we did not have any support from the district attorney's office. At times the job is terrifying, but you do what is necessary and you rely on your training to carry it to fruition. Thankfully, everyone involved escaped any injuries. It could have turned out very differently. (Case Closed by Arrest)

BURGLARY OF STAMPER'S FAMILY MARKET

At approximately 0705 hours, on the morning of August 31, 1988, I received a call from Wayne Stamper, owner/operator of Stamper's Family Market. Mr. Stamper told me a burglary had occurred during the night and entry to the store had been gained by breaking out the large plate glass window just west of the entry door. He said after the burglar(s) made entry to the store they broke out another plate glass window, which allowed them to gain entry into the pharmacy. The pharmacy was located inside, and toward the middle of the store. It was always securely locked, separately from the store, when the business was closed. Mr. Stamper said the shelves in the pharmacy were nearly emptied of drugs and medicines and a lot of the drugs taken were narcotics.

The store had installed a very elaborate alarm system the previous year. The system was set up to call different phone numbers in the case of a forced entry or a fire. The police phone was the first number it would call. Sensors were located on every window and on every door on the exterior of the store, as well as on the man door and plate glass windows in the pharmacy. On the night of the burglary, the alarm had not been set prior to the store being closed. This oversight gave the burglar(s) adequate time to do their bidding. Had the alarm been set, the police would have been alerted when the plate glass window had been broken on the front of the store and we could have possibly prevented the destruction and theft that took place. Because of the alarm system, in a previous case, we did catch a burglar inside the store.

After receiving the call, I immediately called Officer Jerry Lewis and told him about the burglary and I directed him to meet me at the store. Upon arriving at the store, we first took a series of photographs of the entry and of the pharmacy with its broken plate glass window and its emptied shelves. I then asked Mr. Stamper to accompany me throughout the store so he could point out any items that had been moved. We were also looking for any empty spaces, where items may have been and could have been taken by the burglar(s). We did find some beer had been taken from the liquor store and we found items missing in random places throughout the store. Some items were found on the floor, having been knocked off the shelves by the burglar(s). Each location was photographed and logged.

Inside the pharmacy there was a lot of broken glass, both in and out of the room. Numerous bottles and boxes of medicines were found to be on the floor. The shelves, where the drugs were kept, were nearly bare. A small pry bar was lying on the desk, which was located just inside the room below where the plate glass was broken. Mr. Stamper said the pry bar resembled the pry bars he had in the hardware department of the store. He concluded the bar was most likely used to break the glass in the pharmacy. We photographed the pharmacy area and took a lot of notes prior to collecting many of the items as evidence.

Mr. Stamper said a round, white plastic waste paper basket, was missing and its contents were observed to have been poured out on the floor. It was assumed the burglar(s) took the plastic waste paper basket to carry out the drugs they took from the pharmacy. Mr. Stamper also told us the main door into the pharmacy had been left open approximately 4 inches by the intruder(s), which would indicate they left through that door. Officer Lewis dusted the door knob for fingerprints.

Officer Lewis also dusted for fingerprints at the front window area, where entry was originally made, and in other areas of the pharmacy. Anywhere it was evident the burglar(s) had handled items, Officer Lewis attempted to get fingerprints. The pharmacy shelves, where the drugs were stored, were also dusted for fingerprints. Photographs were taken of all the areas where items had been moved.

Throughout the investigation numerous items, which were in locations other than where they had been originally kept, were taken as evidence. These items would most probably have been handled by the burglar(s). One of the items which had been handled, and was taken as evidence, was a plastic money tray. It had been kept inside the desk just outside the pharmacy, and it was found on the floor behind the desk.

An Insulin syringe box, containing thirty syringes, was found sitting on a case of beer near the rear door of the store. These items had to have been handled by the intruder(s). Both were photographed and taken as evidence so they could later be sent to the Alaska State Troopers crime laboratory. The beer was removed from the carton and only the beer carton was taken as evidence. The syringes came from the Pharmacy and the case of beer had been taken from the liquor store. The burglar(s) must have forgotten the items after moving them to an area near the back door.

Most of the morning was spent documenting evidence, photographing the areas where items had been moved or taken, and dusting for fingerprints. We collected and tagged fifteen items which we would be packaging and taking to the Alaska State Trooper laboratory for analysis. We also were able to lift 16 fingerprints that would also be analyzed by the laboratory. NOTE: *The Alaska State Trooper crime laboratory handled all evidence for all the police department's in Alaska.*

After the evidence was collected and all the photographs were taken, I informed Mr. Stamper we were finished collecting evidence and he could do whatever was necessary to secure the building. He said he had called a local carpenter who was going to come in and put plywood over the plate glass window in the front of the store. He said the pharmacy would not be open until the window was replaced and he could restock the items which were taken. I asked Mr. Stamper to figure out the costs of the damage to the store, as well as the replacement cost of everything taken, including the pharmaceuticals, so I could get a ballpark figure of his loss. I would need this when, and if, we caught the burglar and took him/them before the court. I would be asking for restitution in this case.

Throughout the rest of the week I kept busy preparing the evidence and the necessary paperwork needed by the AST laboratory. The case file was getting larger and larger as the days passed. I was able to get the evidence ready for the laboratory by the first of the following week. I caught an airplane and personally hand carried the 15 pieces of evidence, and the fingerprint evidence, to the AST laboratory in Anchorage. The lab stays very busy and they were perpetually under-staffed so, we could only hope they could get to our evidence in a timely manner. When I inquired how long they thought it would be before we would have some results, I was told they would get to it as soon as possible but it could be two to three weeks.

Following my delivering the items to the laboratory, I visited the State Troopers at the AST headquarters. Headquarters was located on the same property as the laboratory and, as always, I was welcomed with open arms. Following my visit with the Alaska State Troopers I returned to the airport, boarded an airplane and returned to Seldovia.

We continued to work the burglary. Other calls for assistance, as well as other criminal complaints, continued coming in and each of them had to be addressed, as well. Just because you have a major case you're working, the day to day operations of the department still have to be addressed. The day to day operations did slow down the investigation somewhat but the burglary was a priority. However, the other citizen complaints are also important and had to be dealt with. We continued to work hard on investigating the burglary and this led to some very long days.

The word about the burglary spread throughout town quickly and we received numerous phone calls from people who shared their thoughts and suspicions, but we never really got anything solid to follow up on.

We did receive a break in the case when my daughter, Donica, called me from the John Cabot cannery, where she was a secretary. She told me a friend of hers had approached her and told her she had been told by a male cannery worker he was planning on breaking into the store. She said this had occurred only a couple days prior to the burglary. My daughter gave me the man's name but I was not acquainted with him. I pulled my daughter's friend in and interviewed her on record and asked what she had heard. She called the man by name and said he had been drinking and he told her he was going to break into the store. She said this was only a couple of days before the actual burglary took place. She said she didn't know the man well, and really didn't know why he told her about it at all. She said she had a friend with her, who had overheard him, and she gave me her friend's name. She said the man sounded like he was bragging, or being macho when he told her of his plans.

I pulled the second lady in, who had reportedly overheard the conversation, and interviewed her, as well. She stated she had been present when the man told them he was planning to break into the store. She also said she wasn't that good a friend to the man and it must have been the liquor that prompted him to talk to them. After she had heard about the burglary, she remembered the conversation and was going to report it but she hadn't had time before I contacted her.

I picked up the suspect and took him to the police department and read him his Miranda rights. He signed a waiver of rights form and I questioned him on record about the burglary. He denied any knowledge, stating he hadn't heard there had been a burglary. He denied telling anyone he was planning to break into the store and stated he didn't know why anyone would say that about him. When I asked where he was on the night in question, he told me he was in the bars until they closed then he'd gone home. He said he lived alone in a room at the cannery bunkhouse and he didn't have anyone who could verify his story. He said he really didn't remember too much as he was very drunk. He said he would have remembered breaking into the store, if he'd done it, but he didn't have anything to do with it. I didn't have enough evidence to hold him at this time but I did ask him if he would let me roll his fingerprints. He reluctantly agreed and I fingerprinted him. I then told him he was free to go but, if he was planning to leave town, I wanted to know about it. He said he was working at the cannery and wasn't going anywhere as long as they were processing.

When we interview a suspect, we ask questions in a certain way in hopes it will bring out the truth. The body language of a suspect also plays into the conclusions an officer makes during the interview. It was my opinion, after conducting the interview with the suspect, he was not being completely truthful with me. He kept his arms crossed throughout the interview and he had a tendency to look down our look away when asked a direct question regarding the burglary. He was nervous throughout the interview and he didn't show the emotion an innocent man should show. When a person is innocent of a crime he is alleged to have committed, he will often become angry or irritable because he feels he's being railroaded. This was not the case with this suspect. He was overly friendly, trying to convince me he wouldn't do such a thing as commit a burglary. I found suspects who are guilty, usually come off as very friendly. This was the case with this suspect. I felt confident I would be having more dealings with the man as this case progressed.

On September 3, 1988, at approximately 1600 hours, I received a call from a lady who said she and her daughter were walking on Spring Street, near the Inside Beach, when she observed a blanket in the ditch, on the east side of the roadway. She said an empty Nally's Dipper potato chip bag was lying beside the blanket and, upon checking further, she found numerous cartons and bottles of drugs inside the blanket. She said she felt they were most probably from the burglary of the store. I asked if I could pick her up and she could show me where the blanket and drugs were found and she said she'd be at the post office. I picked her up and she took me to the location. I photographed the blanket with the drugs and potato chip bag and I collected the items as evidence. I took the lady back to the post office, thanked her for her help, and then took the evidence to the police department. I locked the evidence in the evidence room for later identification. I counted the items before I secured them in the evidence room and found there were one hundred sixty-nine items in all, which included the potato chip bag and the blanket.

At approximately 1255 hours, on September 4, 1988 I received a call from another lady who told me she had been walking home on a trail, near the Inside Beach, and found a lot of drugs dumped in the middle of the trail. She said she was almost sure the drugs were from the store burglary. I asked her if she would show me the location of the drugs and she said she would. I responded to her residence and picked her up and she guided me to the trail where the drugs were dumped. Upon reaching the location, I observed numerous bottles and boxes of drugs spread out on the trail and it appeared they had been spread out and had been gone through. A white waste paper basket, resembling the waste paper basket previously described by Mr. Stamper, was also on the trail. A number of quarters were found, as well. The drugs were photographed and handled as evidence when they were collected. After dropping the lady back at her residence, the drugs, and other evidence, were taken to the police department and secured in the evidence room. There were ninety-one pieces of evidence collected from the trail. I would be going through the items and would be identifying and recording each of them. I would also be packaging them for mailing to the AST laboratory. Hopefully we would be getting a positive identification off some of the items I had already delivered to the Lab and we wouldn't need to send these. We'd have to wait and see.

At approximately 1020 hours on September 21, 1988, I received a telephone call from a latent examiner at the Alaska State Trooper laboratory and he told me eight fingerprints had been identified as prints belonging to my suspect. He said three fingerprints had been found on the syringe box, which we had located near the rear door of the store, and two had been found on the beer container, which was also located in the same location. The other three fingerprints had been found on the plastic coin tray, which had been located behind the desk, just to the rear of the pharmacy. The fingerprint examiner said they were continuing to work the evidence I'd submitted but knew I needed to know the suspect, whose name I'd submitted with the evidence, was identified as handling the aforementioned items. He told me a lot of the items submitted had prints on them but the ridge detail was insufficient for identification purposes.

Upon finding the laboratory had identified my suspect, I called the district attorney's office in Kenai and laid out the case for them. I was told Wayne Stamper and I would have to travel to Kenai on Friday, September 23, 1988, to testify before the Grand Jury. The DA said the laboratory fingerprint technician could testify telephonically from Anchorage. So, arrangements were made for Mr. Stamper and me to go to Kenai. I kept a private vehicle in Homer and we planned to utilize it to drive to Kenai.

Needless to say, I felt good about the case. We had worked it hard and now we had a suspect we were taking before the Grand Jury. I felt positive we'd get a true bill. The DA said we would be charging burglary in the second degree and theft in the second degree, both C class felonies.

Mr. Stamper and I traveled to Kenai and testified before the Grand Jury. We were given a true bill, and brought the felony charges afore-mentioned. An arrest warrant was ordered for my suspect and I was anxious to return to Seldovia and serve that warrant. I called Officer Lewis and told him the good news and, like me, he was very happy to hear it. (NOTE: *When a case is taken before the grand jury, a decision is made whether or not to accept the charges presented to them by the district attorney. They also decide if the suspect named in the case, should be tried for the charges presented. If they believe there is enough evidence to take the case to trial, and there was sufficient evidence wherein the suspect should be tried, they will award you a TRUE BILL. If they decide there is not enough evidence to warrant a trial, a TRUE BILL is not given. After receiving a true bill, arrest warrants for the suspect, are filed with the court.*)

Mr. Stamper and I drove back to Homer and caught an airplane to Seldovia. After I arrived in town, I called Officer Lewis and told him to meet me at the police department and we would go arrest our suspect. Officer Lewis was more than ready and we traveled to the John Cabot cannery. I contacted my daughter and asked her if the suspect was working. She told me he was and the location of where he should be. Officer Lewis and I found the suspect in the back area of the cannery, where he'd been working in the freezer. I approached him and told him he was under arrest for the burglary of Stamper's Market and I placed him in handcuffs. We walked him back to the front of the cannery and told my daughter he wouldn't be coming in tomorrow for work. I told her, "For that matter, I don't think he'll be coming back to work." I asked her if she could have someone pack up his personal belongings so we could send them with him tomorrow, when he was transferred to the Homer jail. She said she'd talk to the superintendent and see that his belongings were brought to the police department.

The suspect was transported to the police department where he was again given his Miranda warning and this time, he refused to sign the waiver of rights form and was not interviewed. A guard was called and he was booked and placed in a jail cell.

The suspect's personal belongings were brought to the police department, and the following day I transported him to Homer, where he would be held until he was arraigned and bail was set.

When a man is charged with a felony, in this case two felonies, he does not get the opportunity to plead guilty, no contest or not guilty during his arraignment. He is afforded the opportunity to talk to an attorney prior to making a plea. In my suspect's case, he could not afford to hire an attorney so the court appointed a public defender for him. His bail was set at $10,000 cash or corporate bond and a court date was set for his bail review and his trial call hearing. At his trial call hearing he can plead to the charge and, if he pleads not guilty, a trial date is set. If he pleads no contest or guilty to the charges, the Judge will set a sentencing date. Prior to sentencing a thorough background check is done and an investigator contacts member of the community to find out about the defendant. This information is given to the judge to assist in the sentencing of a defendant and is called a pre-sentence report.

In our defendant's case the district attorney and the public defender reached a plea bargain. If the defendant agreed to plead guilty to the burglary, the DA would drop the theft charge. The defendant accepted the plea bargain and pled guilty to burglary in the second degree at his trial call hearing. The defendant was ordered to serve six months in jail, he was ordered to pay $6,083.81 in restitution to Wayne Stamper, he was ordered to abstain from drinking alcohol, he was ordered to undergo alcohol and drug screening and he was given five years' probation.

I was very pleased when we were able to solve the burglary but I always felt there was possibly more than one suspect. I felt this due to all the items which were taken and the destruction which took place. I didn't think one man could, or would, pull this off but I couldn't find any evidence that indicated another party being involved. The defendant never did indicate there was anyone with him, and no other suspects were developed, so I was satisfied we got our burglar and the case was closed. It took a lot of man hours and a lot of cooperation from the community to solve the case. The good news is, it was solved and the guilty party went to jail. (Case Closed by Arrest)

1988, An Interesting and Busy Year

We had a total of seven hundred and twenty-three incidents during 1988. The incidents are a total of all the calls made to the police department which require a response by a police officer. The incident form is the first form in any case investigated, or handled, by the department. Along with all the other requests for assistance, the officers of the Seldovia Police Department conducted numerous investigations. Among the cases investigated were two disorderly conduct reports, four cases of driving without a license, we arrested two people for driving while license revoked, we responded to three domestic violence calls, investigated five automobile accidents, arrested three people for driving while intoxicated, impounded one illegally parked vehicle, dealt with one civil disturbance, wrote one citation for basic speed, investigated two theft reports, took two criminal trespass reports, cited one person for indecent exposure, investigated two burglaries not in a dwelling, made an arrest on an assault with a deadly weapon, charged one man with assault in the fourth degree, charged one man with misconduct involving weapons, made two warrant arrests, investigated one death, charged two men with probation violations, charged one man with misconduct involving a controlled substance in the sixth degree, (marijuana), charged one man with criminal mischief, charged one minor with minor in possession of alcohol, charged one man with furnishing liquor to minors and we dealt with one violation of a court order.

The cases listed are all case file reports that take considerable time to complete. The other actions, other than the case file reports, made up the total of seven hundred and twenty-three police responses, and they are recorded on one page which is known as an incident report. The paperwork in a police department, even the size of the Seldovia Police Department, is never ending. Throughout my career, the city did supply clerical help, when the budget would allow. This was a real blessing, in that it freed up a lot of time Wherein the officers could be out investigating crimes instead of setting at a desk doing paperwork.

Saying Goodbye to 'Ol Pard

Officer Jerry L. Lewis was with me for over seven years and we became great friends, as well as partners in the police department. We were more like brothers than just friends. He always called me "Pard," as I guess he did a lot of people, but it had a special meaning to me. Due to some serious health issues, Jerry had to turn in his resignation. It was very hard for him to admit he was not able to continue doing the job he'd done all of his life. Jerry was in poor physical condition, and had been for some time prior to his giving up his job.

Jerry had a very unique way of dealing with the public. He was very jovial, most of the time, and he could usually quiet a disturbance by just talking with those involved. There were very few incidents in those seven years where Jerry wound up having to be physical with anyone. I remember one call where we were called to break up a bar fight between three parties, two brothers and one other very large fellow. Upon entry I pulled the two brothers aside and Officer Lewis took the big guy outside the bar. I didn't notice he had gone outside, due to my having to deal with the two angry brothers. When I did realize he was outside, I went to check on him. I was worried about him being able to control this big fellow. What I first observed when I walked outside was this big guy hovering over Officer Lewis and telling him he was going to kick his butt. I thought this was going to get ugly and I was really shocked when I heard Officer Lewis laugh at this giant of a man. Jerry didn't miss a beat, and immediately asked the big man if he ever noticed what he was wearing around his waist. Before the guy could respond Jerry told him, "These are not toys. They teach us to *kill* people with these. I'm not going to fight you; I'll just kill you." The big guy was visibly shaken by this and, to my surprise, he backed off. He must have been convinced Officer Lewis wasn't joking. I also had concerns and was thinking, "I think he means it." Either way, nothing more happened and the matter was brought to a peaceful conclusion without having to go hands on with anyone.

When Officer Lewis came to Seldovia from Whitter, he brought a large collection of VHF tapes with him, which he shared with people in the community at no charge. He was the first person to have such a large collection and there were many people who took advantage of his generosity and repeatedly borrowed tapes from him.

Officer Lewis lived in a fifth wheel trailer and he had parked it right next to me in the city trailer park. I lived in a fourteen by seventy-foot mobile home, at the time, and we were always at one another's residence. I distinctly remember one afternoon when Officer Lewis had a very large woman, who he had loaned VHF tapes to in the past, come to his trailer and ask if she could come in and watch a movie with him. Jerry was not interested in a relationship with this woman so, being very quick witted, he told her he'd love to watch a movie with her but his chief, referring to me, wouldn't allow him to have any women in his trailer. This made the woman boiling mad and she immediately stomped out of his trailer and came over next door to my trailer and pounded on my door, nearly knocking it off the hinges.

I had made it a rule in my home, if someone came to the door and knocked hard or aggressively, which was indicative of some sort of problem, I would be the one to answer the door. On this occasion when I opened the door, this large lady started screaming at me, asking me who I thought I was to tell Officer Lewis he couldn't have any women in his trailer. My initial reaction was to argue with her but she didn't give me a chance to say anything. She continued yelling, telling me I couldn't tell Officer Lewis what to do on his off time. She said she was ticked off because I couldn't tell anyone who they can and can't have in their own home. Well, I'm not the brightest bulb on the tree but I figured out, by her onslaught, what Officer Lewis had told her, to avoid having to tell her he wasn't interested in a relationship with her. I thought I'd get even with my old Pard, and I told the lady I was wrong and I would like to apologize to her and to Officer Lewis. I told her to go back and tell Jerry I was sorry and I really didn't mind if he had women in his home, when he was off duty. I told her to also tell him I admitted to her, I'd overstepped my authority by telling him that he couldn't have female visitors. Well, this appeased the lady and she left my home happier than when she'd arrived. Well, my old Pard told me later, he had a heck of a time coming up with another excuse why he couldn't watch a movie with her. I asked him if they had watched a romantic flick but he was adamant they didn't watch any movie together, and he added, no thanks to me. He said he thought I had his back but it was evident I didn't. I told him I couldn't believe he'd use his old Pard as an excuse to get out of watching a movie with that young lady. I have to admit, I did get a lot of mileage out of that one. We both laughed about this after a time but I laughed a little louder than old Pard did.

Officer Lewis was a television addict. He would watch TV on most all of his off-time hours and, at one point, when the nights were quiet, he'd take his little black and white twelve-volt television set with him to work. He'd set in different areas and, while watching for traffic violations and other problems, he'd set the TV on his dash board, plug it into the cigarette lighter socket, and watch a program. This had been going on for about a week or so when I got a call to come into the city manager's office. I responded to the city office and went in to see the manager. I was asked if I knew Officer Lewis was watching TV in his car when he was supposed to be working. I played dumb and the manager told me he thought Officer Lewis was smarter than to park in front of the mayor's house and watch TV while he was on duty. I assured the manager I'd put an end to it and I left the city office. I waited until Officer Lewis was on duty and I pulled him into my office. I ask if he'd really thought about how it'd be received when he was watching his TV when he was supposed to be working. He asked me if I'd gotten a complaint and I told him the mayor must not have liked the program he was watching when he parked in front of her home, because she talked to the city manager about it. He, in turn, had a discussion with me. Officer Lewis found this amusing and could hardly keep from laughing. I told him he had to leave the TV at home from now on and I hoped he'd use better judgement in the future and not screw up in front of the mayor's house. This incident also provided a lot of comments from me for a number of months. I would ask Jerry what TV program he had watched last night while he was patrolling, and he'd just shake his head or walk away.

After Jerry retired, he had to move to Anchorage to be near medical assistance, due to his health problems. He lived for another two years. After he passed away, I traveled to Anchorage and attended his funeral. After getting permission from his brother, I took his uniform to the mortuary and told them the family wanted him buried in it. He was buried in full uniform and was wearing his Seldovia Police Department badge. I know this is what he would have wanted. He looked very peaceful and was not in pain anymore, and for that I am truly grateful. I will always remember Officer Lewis and all the memories I have I will forever cherish. You were like a brother to me and you will never be forgotten. Rest in peace Pard.

EMPLOYEE PROTECTION

I t was the spring of the year 1989, in mid-May. The employees were all going about their different duties and everything seemed to be going well. Personally, I had a pretty rocky relationship with the present city manager and our philosophies were certainly in direct opposition of one another. Under this manager I had been required to jump through a lot of hoops that were, in my opinion, totally unwarranted. Even though I tried to discourage it, he directed me, at one point, to submit a plan for developing a community watch program in Seldovia. As directed, I researched what it would take to implement a community watch program and found, in other areas, the program was funded through donations from local businesses. In doing my research I was told signs would have to be made, to be posted around town, and classes would have to be held for those who wanted to participate in the program. I also found records had to be kept regarding meetings and any reports made by the general public had to be documented. In my opinion, this program was not needed in Seldovia and it would just be an added financial burden to the businesses in our community, and it would create a lot more paperwork for the police department. But, as directed, I put the program together on paper and submitted it, with a written statement in opposition to the implementation of the program in Seldovia. I outlined my reasons I opposed the program and submitted my research within the timeframe the manager had given me. There was always a timeframe I was dealing with when given directives by this city manager, regardless of the caseload or the police department's daily obligations.

The manager also told me he wanted me to set up a meeting with the principal of the school and talk to him about me coming to the school one hour per week to discuss criminal law with the high school students. There were some major problems with this idea being implemented. First, I didn't feel I could be dedicating an hour per week to that type program. I had to stand ready to respond at any given time for police responses and, even though we were not a crime-ridden community, I didn't see where I could actually set aside a given time frame. But more importantly, I was not a teacher and I didn't feel qualified to teach the high school students something I was still learning myself. In an attempt to appease the city manager, I contacted the principal of the school and told him of the managers idea. I also told him of my reluctance to undertake such a program, and my reasonings for not wanting to take on the project. The principle, being a personal friend, told me to tell the city manager he could not set that time aside with the curriculum being what it was. Even though he didn't volunteer the information, I feel the principle was doing me a personal favor by rejecting this program.

The city managers next step was to direct me to bring in all of my certificates of training, any certifications and any records I had relating to any classes I had undertaken. It was very apparent to me he was trying to find something wherein he could terminate me and put someone else in the position as police chief. I was told, and tend to agree, the manager was, most probably, taking his direction from the City Council. I'm sure they felt if they could get myself, and one or two other employees terminated, they would be able to persuade the rest of the employees to vote out the union.

To better understand what the employees were feeling, under his management, I need to back up a few months prior to us becoming union members. On a Friday afternoon, just before quitting time, the city manager called an employee meeting at the city office conference room. All employees were directed to be at that meeting. When we all were gathered, he told us, even though he felt bad about it, a change was about to take place regarding our employment status with the city.

He said on Monday morning either one person would be out of a job or all the employees would be taking a 20% reduction in pay. He went on to say the city was in dire financial difficulties and this was the only way the city could survive. Before dismissing us, he told us he had done everything he could to avoid this but there was no avoiding it. The city would be bankrupt if something did not change immediately.

The employees of the city of Seldovia were a pretty resilient bunch. Following the meeting at the city offices, we gathered outside to discuss our feelings and, to the last employee, we were not ready to lay down and roll over and let this happen, if there was any way to stop it. It was decided everyone would meet at my residence, since I had a larger house than most of the employees, and we would attempt to find some way to avoid what the manager had planned for Monday morning. We all felt rather helpless but hoped we could come up with something which could avoid someone losing their job or all of us taking a 20% cut in pay. I still remember the helpless feelings we all shared at the time.

Most all the employees did meet in my home on Saturday, and we attempted to call a number of different organizations, in hopes they would represent us. The Municipal Employees Association showed no interest, due to our small numbers. I, like the rest of the employees, couldn't personally afford to give up 1/5 of my wages, let alone my job. The city was not known for paying high wages and most all of us were living paycheck to paycheck. After making a number of phone calls to different organizations, with negative results, in desperation we called the International Brotherhood of Electrical Workers, (IBEW). Being a union representing the electrical workers, I can honestly say, we were shocked when they agreed to take on negotiations on our behalf. A vote was taken of all the employees present at this meeting and the vote was unanimous that we all wanted IBEW to represent us. Even though I had never before been a part of a union organization, I was now one of the ring leaders who brought a union to Seldovia. All the employees were new to having representation and all of us were apprehensive. However, we didn't feel we had a choice, after being given no voice in the matter, and knowing what was going to happen Monday morning. We felt this was the only avenue left for us to protect our jobs and/or our wages.

On Monday morning, promptly at 8:00 AM, the City of Seldovia received a call from the IBEW union informing them they were now negotiating for the majority of the employees of the city of Seldovia, and no changes could be made without negotiations first taking place with their organization. The city was told there would be no changes in employment status, no changes in wages and no changes in job descriptions, without first going into negotiations. The employees covered in the IBEW contract included the police department personnel, the public works personnel, the harbormaster and the custodian. The only positions not covered were the city manager and the city office personnel.

This, of course, generated a lot of conversation and turmoil in Seldovia. A special Council meeting was called, which would be held in an executive session. The citizens throughout the community had varied opinions of what was taking place. Many who had been affiliated with unions throughout their employment years were in favor of the union while others, who, for the most part, had not been represented by unions, were opposed to our union affiliation. It seemed everyone voiced their opinions and the town was abuzz with conversations. I'm happy to report, no changes were made on Monday morning and work continued as usual. I was told, however, that myself and a couple other employees, who the administration felt were instrumental in our becoming represented by a union, should be aware, the city would do everything within their power to see to it we were terminated. I was told by some close friends, who had direct one-on-one information, I should personally be very concerned. It was as if a hit was put out on me and I had a target on my back.

Since you now understand the reason for the friction between myself and the city manager, let's get back to the city manager making me jump through hoops. You recall the manager insisted I submit all my certifications and other documentation reference training. As in his other directives, I did as I was told and turned in copies of all my certificates of training and all my certifications by the date he requested. I was curious to see what the city manager's next move would be and within a couple days I got my answer. I received a memo from the him with a number of Alaska state statutes which contained many which he had highlighted. As I read, I found the highlighted statutes were the ones relating to the requirements for police officers in the state of Alaska. As you recall in my first book, I mentioned I had lost the sight in my left eye as a 7-year-old in a farming accident. Even though I had already served nearly 10 years as the police chief for Seldovia, the manager felt I could not legally hold the position, due to the restrictions regarding police officers having correctable vision of 20-15 in each eye. What the manager did not know, and didn't bother to research, was the regulations he had highlighted, applied to a patrol officer and not a chief of police. I had already researched this matter years before this, and found I could legally hold the position as chief of police. This was determined by the Alaska Police Standards Council. After a day or so had passed, I was approached by the manager and asked if I'd had a chance to peruse the statutes that he had sent to me. I answered in the affirmative but didn't give any more of an explanation. When he asked my opinion, I told him, if he had any questions, he should research it and find out for himself. The manager was very smug during our conversation, thinking he had found the answer needed to remove me from office. He knew he had to have all his ducks in a row if he was going to terminate me. I was now represented by the IBEW union and they would be speaking in my behalf. This was a major roadblock for him. I assume, following that conversation, he did contact the Alaska Police Standards Council and was told the statutes were intended for police officers, other than the chief of police. I was not approached again on this matter and, from that time, until he left the manager's position, I was not given any more hoops to jump through. I think he finally decided he was fighting a losing battle and could not find a reason to terminate me. The Alaska Police Standards Council looked at the chief of police position as being an administrative position, and in most larger departments, this is the case. This distinction by the Alaska Police Standards Council enabled me to hold the office as a chief of police.

Many people, even today, question why a small group of people, who were employed by the City of Seldovia, would request union affiliation. Hopefully this clarifies any questions you may have regarding this matter. At times, due to the actions by an administration beyond our control, one does have to call on big brother for assistance.

It was only a couple months later when the city manager gave his resignation and left the office. I don't believe any of the employees of the city regretted his decision. No one threw him a going away party and I don't believe any of the employees expressed their disappointment in his decision to go.

I guess, given the circumstances today, I owe that city manager a debt of gratitude. Because of his actions, and his unorthodox management style, the city employees became affiliated with the IBEW union and, because the union made available a retirement program to its members, I now enjoy a monthly check for the rest of my retirement years. Up until that point there was no retirement available through the City of Seldovia for any of the employees. Upon becoming affiliated with the IBEW union, we were able to get a retirement program, no one lost their job and no one's wages were cut by 20% that following Monday morning. Even though we became union, and no changes were made, the city did not go bankrupt, as the city manager had predicted, and, as of this writing, on the 17th day of April, 2020, we are still functioning as an incorporated 1st class city in the State of Alaska. Following my retirement from the city, and the departure of most of the original employees, who were covered by the union agreement, new city employees filling the positions, voted the union out. I hope they do not regret their decision. Myself, and the employees during the time we were affiliated with the union, repeatedly found their representation to be invaluable. Time and time again the union came to the aid of an employee. I certainly do not regret the decision, which was made in my home on that Saturday, many years ago, when we chose to join the International Brotherhood of Electrical Workers Union.

DWI, Following a Motor Vehicle Accident

At approximately 2110 hours, June 17, 1989, I received a report from a citizen that a vehicle was in a ditch in the area of mile four, Jakolof Bay Road, and it was lying on its side. The caller told me who the vehicle belonged to, but said there was no one around when they had stopped to check to see if anyone was injured.

I responded to mile four, Jakolof Bay Road, and found a tan Suburban lying on its side in a ditch. No one was around the vehicle but footprints were observed walking away from the scene. I immediately knew who owned the vehicle and I wondered what had become of him. I went to two of the homes near where the accident had occurred but neither of the residents had seen the owner of the vehicle. The one lady I talked to stated she had heard something, approximately one hour before I contacted her, and she thought this may have been when the accident occurred.

I returned to the scene of the accident and took a series of photographs of the area and of the vehicle. It was evident the vehicle had hit the snow berm on the north side of the roadway, had then turned one hundred eighty degrees, hit the snow berm a second time and had gone over the berm, coming to rest on the right side, or passenger's side, of the vehicle. The windshield was broken out and the window on the rear right door was also broken. I checked the temperature of the engine and it was warm, but not hot, so I concluded the accident had occurred between one to two hours before I arrived.

While I was investigating the scene of the accident, a vehicle headed out the road, stopped and told me the owner of the Suburban was observed walking into town at approximately the two-mile marker. I immediately headed toward town in hopes of locating the driver. As I was approaching 1.5 mile, I saw the vehicle owner walking down the middle of the roadway. I stopped the police vehicle and approached the man on foot. I noticed he was not wearing his glasses or hat, which he always wore. I also observed a scrape type injury on the right side of his face. I smelled a strong odor of alcohol coming from him and, when he spoke, I noticed he was slurring his words. His eyes were bloodshot and he was unsteady on his feet. I asked if he was injured in the accident and he told me he was fine. He said he was returning to Seldovia from Jakolof Bay, where he'd taken a person to catch a boat. He said he'd clipped the snow berm on the side of the road and lost control of his vehicle. When I asked what happened to his glasses and hat, he told me he didn't know and he'd probably lost them in the accident.

I put the man through a number of field sobriety tests including the American alphabet, a balance test, asked him to count backwards and I showed him how to correctly do the heel to toe test. He attempted, but failed each of the tests. I informed him he was under arrest for driving while intoxicated and I placed him in handcuffs. He asked if we could go check for his glasses in his vehicle so I turned around and took him back to the scene. I took the handcuffs off and let him enter his vehicle to look for his glasses. In a few minutes he returned to the patrol vehicle wearing his glasses and his hat. I told him to have a seat in the front passenger side of the vehicle and I didn't put him in handcuffs again. He was not combative and was very amenable to my directions so I didn't see a need to restrain him again.

Upon reaching the police department, I read the man his Miranda warning and he signed his waiver of rights form and I interviewed him on record. When I asked him to tell me what had happened, he told me he'd taken a lady to Jakolof and he'd drank a couple beers and had a couple shots of whiskey before starting back to Seldovia. He said he really didn't think he was too intoxicated to be driving when he had the accident. He then said he really didn't remember the accident and really didn't remember too much after leaving Jakolof Bay. He said he had a fifth of whiskey with him, which was approximately half full and, following the accident, he sat in a driveway near four mile, Jakolof Bay Road, and drank the rest of the whiskey in about fifteen minutes. He said he was alone in the vehicle at the time of the accident and, even though his face was scratched, he was not injured in the accident.

I administered an intoximeter breath test at 2235 hours which resulted in a finding of .185 blood alcohol content. The booking procedure was done and the man was locked in a jail cell. A jail guard was called in to guard the prisoner the rest of the night.

After signing a promise to appear for his arraignment, I released the man on his own recognizance at approximately 1000 hours the next morning.

At his arraignment the man pled not guilty and ask for a public defender. The judge asked a series of questions regarding his employment, his account balances and cash on hand and then appointed the public defender to represent him.

The case was set for trial and a date for the calendar call was set. At calendar call the man pled "no contest" after the driving while intoxicated charges were reduced to reckless driving. He was fined $500 with $250 suspended, ordered to undergo alcohol screening at SKIAP, his operator's license was revoked for ninety days, he was placed on probation for one year and was told he couldn't violate any criminal laws while he was on probation.

The district attorney told me he'd had to reduce the charges from DWI to reckless driving because the man stated he'd consumed one half bottle of whiskey immediately following the accident and we couldn't prove otherwise. Having to reduce the sentence didn't really bother me that much, even though I felt the man was drunk when he had the accident. I really didn't know, but thought he may be using the consumption of the whiskey after the accident, as an excuse for his high blood alcohol content. However, he did come across as truthful when he told me about consuming the one-half bottle of whiskey following the accident. He still was sentenced wherein he had to pay a fine and undergo alcohol screening. I did my job and I was satisfied with the outcome. (Case Close by Arrest)

ASSAULT WITH A DEADLY WEAPON

At approximately 1040 hours on June 6,1989, I was approached by a man who stated he wanted to press charges against a man, who we'll call Charles, for assault with a deadly weapon. He said Charles approached his vehicle while he and a friend were parked in the parking lot at the Seldovia Lodge. The victim stated Charles shoved a knife through the passenger side window and was waiving it in his face and threatening to cut his heart out. The passenger, who was with the victim, told me he was present during the altercation and Charles reached across in front of him toward the victim with the knife, and the way he was swinging the knife around, he thought he was going to get cut. I directed the victim and his friend to meet me at the police department because I wanted to get this on record.

I interviewed the victim on record at the police department and he told me he and Charles had been working on a boat the victim had recently purchased. He said they had gotten into an argument, while at the Seldovia Lodge a few days prior. He said Charles became angry and had reached across the table and grabbed him by the collar. This developed into a wrestling match and both men went to the floor. He told me there were no punches thrown and no one was hit but Charles said his ribs were hurt in the scuffle. The victim said he didn't believe Charles was injured in the scuffle because it didn't amount to much more than a wrestling match and no one hit anyone. He said the altercation in the parking lot started after he asked Charles why he hadn't been to work on the boat. Charles told him he'd come back to work when he was good and ready and then he got angry and pulled the knife and threatened him.

The passenger, who was present with the victim at the time of the incident, was also interviewed on record. He told me the victim had observed Charles drive in and park in the parking lot at the Seldovia Lodge. The victim waited for Charles to exit the vehicle then asked him why he hadn't been to work on the boat. Charles became angry and was yelling at the victim, accusing the victim of hurting his ribs, and then he pulled the knife. He pushed the knife through the passenger window, and across in front of the passenger, to within 6 inches of the victim's shoulder. Charles told the victim he was going to cut his heart out. The passenger said he was also fearful of getting cut, the way Charles was waving the knife around. He said the victim started to exit the vehicle and Charles put the knife away and walked up to the Seldovia Lodge. The passenger concluded his interview by stating he and the victim were both in fear of getting cut.

On June 6, 1989, at approximately 1230 hours, I arrested Charles, after locating him on Kachemak Street. When I searched him, I found a Gerber folding knife, with a bone handle, and a utility knife. Both knives were taken as evidence. Also found on his person was a metal pipe, commonly known as a pot pipe, which had vegetable matter in it. It was also taken as evidence.

At approximately 1243 hours, June 6, 1989, following his Miranda warning being read and his signing of the waiver of rights form, Charles was interviewed and his statement was recorded. He said he and the victim had gotten into an altercation at the Seldovia Lodge three or four days ago, and the victim had come across the table and had grabbed him. He told me the owner of the Seldovia Lodge had witnessed the altercation. Charles then said he and the victim had another argument today, in the parking lot at the Seldovia Lodge. He said the victim was saying he was going to finish the fight, which had started three or four days ago. Charles said he thought he might have a broken rib from the previous altercation, and he pulled the knife in self-defense. He wasn't going to let the victim hurt him again, he said.

I asked if he had threatened the victim by shoving the knife at him through the passenger window of the victim's vehicle and he admitted he did. He said he didn't know how close the knife was to the victim, or to his passenger, but he wasn't going to be hurt anymore by the victim. He told me he had a doctor's appointment so x-rays could be taken to ascertain if his rib was broken or not. He said nothing more happened and he then left and walked up to the Lodge.

Following the interview, I put Charles through the booking process and locked him in a jail cell. A jail guard was called and came in to guard him.

After the guard arrived, I responded to the Seldovia Lodge and interviewed the owner and recorded that conversation, as well. I told him Charles told me he had witnessed the first altercation between he and the victim. The owner said he had witnessed it and the argument started over the victim saying something about his boat needing some bearings of some kind. Charles told him it didn't need the bearings and an argument began. The Lodge owner told me the victim came across the table at Charles and they went to the floor, wrestling with one another. He said he broke it up, telling the two to take it outside and not to tear up the dining room. He said it really didn't amount to too much and he didn't think much more about it.

I returned to the police department following my interview with the Seldovia Lodge owner and had the guard bring Charles out of the jail cell and into my office. After signing a promise to appear form and, after agreeing to have no contact with the victim, I released Charles on his own and recognizance. I warned him that any contact with the victim would result in his being arrested again, but he wouldn't be released on his own recognizance next time. I told him a high bail would be requested and he'd still be held to the no contact restriction. He assured me he wouldn't have any contact with the victim.

I submitted the case to the district attorney charging assault in the third degree on both the victim and his passenger but the district attorney reduced the charges to one assault in the fourth degree and Charles pled guilty to it. The district attorney said the victim had not been totally honest regarding the first altercation, in that he was the aggressor and had stated the suspect was the one who grabbed him first. I argued that, regardless, two people were placed in fear of imminent physical injury, after being accosted with a deadly weapon. My arguments fell on deaf ears. I really wanted a lengthy sentence on Charles because he had a couple other Felonies in his past. He was one of the people we arrested and charged in our sting operations for selling Marijuana to our Confidential Informant. I also brought this up to the district attorney but I may as well have saved my breath.

Charles pled no contest to the misdemeanor charge of assault in the fourth degree, and he was fined $500.00 with $250.00 suspended, he was put on probation for one year and the knife, the utility knife and the pot pipe became property of the Seldovia police department.

In my opinion, this was not even close to what should have happened in this case and I strongly feel if the same scenario were to take place in Homer, Kenai, Soldotna, Ninilchik or Seward, Charles would have been charged with both felonies and would have received a substantial sentence including a great deal of jail time. Sometimes an officer asks himself, why do I put so much effort into these cases when I have little, or no control, of even what charges to file? Well, it must be the fourteen miles of water between Seldovia and the road system. It must cost too much to pursue any cases in Seldovia, short of homicide. Do I sound disgruntled? Well, I was. It was very discouraging and I couldn't see it ever changing. (Case Closed by Arrest)

SEXUAL ASSAULT AND ASSAULT
FOURTH DEGREE

On June 23, 1989, at approximately 0230 hours, I received a call from a lady who stated she had been assaulted by her live-in boyfriend. She said he had come home intoxicated, after the bars had closed, and was angry. She told me she tried to leave and he stopped her and dragged her back into the house by the hair. She further stated he had kicked her in the stomach and in the back. She said he hit her and slapped her repeatedly. She told me she was at SKIAP now, and was safe. I asked if she needed medical attention and she said she didn't think so. She said she'd see how she felt in the morning. She said she wanted to report the assault and would come in and see me at the police department at 0900 hours.

At approximately 0853 hours the lady came to the police department and I interviewed her on record with the conversation being tape recorded. She told me her boyfriend had arrived home around 0030 hours and he was intoxicated and argumentative. She said they got into an argument and he asked her things like, "You want to get tough with me." She said she was frightened and ran out of the trailer they lived in, trying to get away. She was running down the driveway when he caught up to her and dragged her back into the trailer by the hair, she said. When she would fall down, he would kick her in the back and in the stomach. He was slapping her when she would be getting up and he was hitting her with his fist, and she said he threatened to kill her. When he got her inside the trailer, he made her undress so she wouldn't run out of the house again. After she had disrobed, he forced her to perform oral sex on him and she said she was so frightened, she went along with it. At one point she said he told her he would kill her if she didn't' perform the sex act. She said she thought he might calm down and, finally, he did pass out and she was able to get dressed and escaped with the vehicle. She said she did the janitorial work at SKIAP, and had a key, and she thought she'd be safe there.

Following the interview, I called women's services in Homer, requesting they assist the victim in obtaining a temporary restraining order (TRO). I then encouraged her to be examined by the doctor and she asked if I'd call Dr. Larry Reynolds and make an appointment for her. I called Doctor Reynolds and he told me to have her come over and he'd examine her right away.

Due to the seriousness of this case, I called the Alaska State Troopers to let them know what had taken place. Their residence was outside the city limits in trooper territory and, even though I had a trooper's commission and handled their cases in our area, I thought they needed to be involved in this one. I talked with Sgt. Tom Sumey and he made arrangements for Trooper Franko D'Angelo to come to Seldovia to assist in the case. The trooper arrived in Seldovia at approximately 1350 hours and I picked him up and briefed him on what had taken place up to this point. I had located the suspect in the Linwood Bar, prior to picking up Trooper D'Angelo, and we drove to the bar to see if the suspect would accompany us to the police department for an interview. Upon entering the bar, I spotted the suspect sitting at the end of the bar. We approached him and observed he had a drink setting in front of him. We told him there had been a complaint that we needed to talk to him about. It was at that time we noticed his voice was slurred and he was showing signs of intoxication. When he stood up to accompany us, he was very unsteady on his feet and had to hold onto the bar to maintain his balance. I asked the bartender what the suspect was drinking and he told me it was tequila. I admonished the bartender, telling him the man was too intoxicated to be in a bar, let alone to be served alcohol. I asked to see the manager and the bartender called her down from upstairs. The manager told me she gave directions telling the bartender not to serve him and she was not happy he had not followed her orders.

The suspect was taken to the Seldovia police department and was interviewed on record, and the conversation was tape recorded. Trooper D'Angelo read the suspect his Miranda warning and he signed the waiver of rights form. The suspect denied assaulting the victim, but at one point in the interview, he did state she had run out to the truck and had gone after her, but he said she slammed the door and was gone. He never did admit to hitting, kicking or slapping her and he would not admit to dragging her back into the trailer by her hair. He further denied any oral sex took place. Additional interviewing failed to bring out any confessions by the suspect, other than when he said he did run out to the truck after the victim. He, up until that point, stated she had not run out trying to escape. After attempting over and over to get the suspect to admit to the assault on the victim, the interview was ended and the suspect was arrested and booked into the Seldovia jail. A guard was called in to watch the prisoner while the Trooper and I continued to investigate the allegations.

Our first stop was the clinic where we talked with Dr. Larry Reynolds. He told us the victim had signed a release of information form, allowing him to divulge to us what his examination had revealed. He said he had found abrasions on the left side of her chin and bruising on the right side of her chin, which were fresh and consistent with someone being repeatedly hit with an open hand or a fist. He said her hair was matted and some was missing, which was indicative of her hair having been pulled repeatedly or, as indicated in the victim's statements, of her being dragged by the hair. The doctor said he found bruising on the arm, which was consistent with her stating she had been pulled back into the house. He said he'd also found a linear abrasion on her abdomen, which could have come from being kicked in the stomach. She had been struck in the head hard enough to raise a knot, he said. She had reportedly been forced to have oral sex with the suspect but the doctor said his examination had no way of proving this had, or had not, occurred. The trooper asked the doctor for a written report and he said he'd provide it through my office and he'd include the release of information form.

We next stopped and interviewed the taxi driver, who had driven the suspect home the night before. She told us the suspect was very intoxicated and was in a bad mood. She said there were two other female occupants in the cab, who were also being taken home after bar closure, and the suspect was hitting on them during the ride out the road.

Trooper D'Angelo and I then returned to the police department and he was given copies of the taped interview I had conducted with the victim. I then transported the trooper, and the suspect, to the airport, where they took a Homer Air flight to Homer.

Following the trooper's departure, I responded to the Linwood Bar to locate the bartender who had served the suspect. I wrote him a citation for serving an intoxicated person on licensed premises. He pled guilty at his arraignment and was fined $500 with $250 suspended and he was placed on probation for one year. I'm sure the judge made a point of telling him he would be hit with a much harsher sentence if there was a repeated offense.

The assault and sexual assault case were turned over to the Alaska State Troopers at that point and the suspect was charged with a domestic violence assault in the fourth degree and he ultimately pled no contest to the charges. Due to his extensive criminal record, he received two years in jail with eighteen months suspended, leaving six months to serve. He was served with a temporary restraining order and was given a fine of $500 with $200 suspended and was placed on probation for five years. He was also ordered to undertake alcohol screening upon his release from jail. The sexual assault could not be charged because of no evidence to support the allegations.

A criminal background was requested on the suspect and he was found to have a DWI, two assaults, one murder, two thefts and a burglary in his background. He had served a lot of jail time. He served three days on the DWI, sixteen years on the murder and six years for the burglary.

Once in a while we run across a really bad guy and this suspect would fall into that category. It seemed he had to continue his criminal lifestyle. I often wondered what kind of upbringing someone like this had, which could have turned him to taking up crime as a way of life. I certainly don't have the answers, but every once in a while, I ran across one. I felt good when I could get a bad guy off the streets. I don't consider myself naïve but I find it hard to believe how some people could treat others so badly. These people are the main reason there are police officers out there doing their level best to protect the majority of the population. Most people are good, honest, hardworking folks, who are just trying to make a decent living. What is sad is that ten percent of the population causes ninety nine percent of the problems and the majority of these problems result from alcohol or drug abuse. Take drugs and alcohol out of the equation and the cop on the street would have a dream job. (Case Closed by Arrest)

Assault with a Deadly Weapon, Two Counts

On September 6. 1989, at approximately 0326 hours, I received a call from the 911 operator reporting an assault with a deadly weapon at a residence on Jakolof Bay Road. I called Officer John Gruber and told him to gear up and I would pick him up and I explained what was reported. I left my residence and called Homer police dispatch, letting them know we were responding. Before I reached Officer Gruber's residence to pick him up, a second call was made to the 911 operator from the same caller, reporting someone was going to die if the police didn't get there soon. The caller, the neighbor who lived next door, told Homer dispatch, two shots had been heard coming from next door and there was screaming and it sounded like items were being broken.

Officer Gruber and I arrived on scene at approximately 0342 hours. It was very dark and we parked at the end of the driveway and walked up to the residence. The lights were on in the residence and we observed the windows to be broken out and numerous items had been thrown out into the yard. The suspect could be seen inside the residence throwing items around. Upon approaching the home, the man who called, and the female victim who lived at the home, were standing outside and they told us to be careful, informing us the man was going crazy. Both Officer Gruber and I drew our weapons and I called out to the man, knowing him personally, and told him who I was and that I was coming in. The suspect yelled for me to come on in and he said he wouldn't fight with the Police. The door was ajar and he was visible to both I and Officer Gruber. I could see he didn't have anything in his hands and I told him to raise his hands above his head. Upon his doing so, Officer Gruber and I entered the residence. I advised the man he was under arrest and he put his hands behind his back and turned around to be handcuffed, without being told. I observed what appeared to be blood on the man's hand and I asked if he needed medical attention. He said he was fine and he didn't need any help. I smelled a slight odor of alcohol on the man's breath but he didn't' show any signs of impairment. He may have drunk just enough to lesson his inhibitions to make it easier to come here to do what he'd done. As soon as the man was in custody his estranged wife, the female victim, asked, from outside the residence, if she could come in an get her two children. I told her she could and she entered the residence and went down the hall to the boy's bedroom. Up until that point, I was unaware that anyone else was inside the residence. The lady came out of the bedroom with her 2½ year old and her 8-month-old boys. Both were crying and were frightened from all that had been taking place. She left the residence with the two children and told me she'd be next door if she was needed for anything.

We found the residence to be a total disaster. Everything was thrown around and a lot of items were broken. The TV, stereo and other electronic items, which had been in a large entertainment center, were on the floor and the entertainment center was turned over as well. Some of the items were observed to be broken. All the windows in the living room area were broken out, including the two large plate glass windows. The cupboards had been opened and everything thrown onto the floor. The kitchen table was upside down and the couch was lying on its back. There was broken glass everywhere in the kitchen and living room areas. It was very apparent the suspect had been on a rampage for quite some time prior to our arrival.

I asked Officer Gruber to stay at the residence and see that no one else came in, or took anything, until we had a chance to go through the crime scene. I told him I was going to transport the suspect to town and get him booked into jail. I also was going to conduct an interview with the suspect, if he would talk to me, and I told Officer Gruber it might take a while before I returned to collect evidence. He told me to take my time and said he he'd guard the place until I returned.

I transported the suspect to the police department and, when we arrived, I read him his Miranda warning but he refused to be interviewed. I told him now was his chance to tell his side of the story but he still refused the interview. I booked him and locked him in the jail cell. I called a jail guard to come in and guard the suspect. When the guard arrived, I told him to closely watch the suspect because he could be suicidal. He was despondent and had been drinking. He was also having marital problems and often people feel there is no reason to continue living when they are having these type stresses in their lives. I wanted to take any steps necessary to keep anything from happening.

I got my 35 MM camera, with extra film, and I took the movie camera and drove back to the residence. When I reached the residence, I filmed every room in the house and the outer area, where a number of items had been thrown out through the broken windows. I took both still shots and a movie of the areas. A small hole, resembling a bullet hole, was observed in the ceiling of the bedroom and another small hole was found in the entry door. Still another hole was also observed in the entry door, but it was felt it was made with something other than a bullet, due to its square shape. The male victim, the man who was with the female victim during the assault, had returned to the residence in my absence, and had given Officer Gruber the rifle he said the suspect used when he had threatened him and his girlfriend. It was a .270 caliber Winchester model 700, and it had a Bushnell custom six power scope on it. The rifle was taken into evidence, as was an empty .270 caliber cartridge, which was located in the hallway of the residence. Another empty cartridge was found in the chamber of the rifle. Four more rounds, unfired, were found to be in the magazine of the bolt action rifle. Also located in the residence was the suspect's coveralls, which he must have taken off upon entry. In the front pockets were a set of keys to the four-wheeler he'd ridden to within three tenths of a mile of the house. A metal sight cover was found in the master bedroom, by the bed, and two homemade scope covers were located in the living room, near the entry to the hallway. These items were all taken as evidence.

The female victim was contacted at the neighbor's residence and an interview, on record, was conducted and a voice recording was made of the conversation. She told me her boyfriend had arrived at her residence shortly after midnight and they had watched television for a little while then had gone to bed, going to sleep around 0130 hours. Her two children, two-and-a-half years and eight-months, were sleeping in their bedroom when all this occurred. She and her soon to be ex-husband, the suspect, had separated and were getting a divorce and he was not happy she had a new boyfriend. She said something awakened her and she looked up to see the silhouette of someone standing in her bedroom, and pointing a rifle at her and her boyfriend. The suspect was alleged to have yelled he was going to kill them both. She said she jumped out of bed and grabbed the rifle by the barrel and was trying to get it away from the suspect when her boyfriend awoke and jumped up and grabbed the rifle. She said she let go and her boyfriend and the suspect were wrestling for the rifle when it went off and the bullet went through the ceiling of the bedroom. She said she had turned loose of the weapon when her boyfriend had grabbed it and she ran out into the living room. The two continued to wrestle over the weapon and wound up in the living room area of the house. They knocked the couch over when they went over it and wound up on the floor. The suspect somehow had ejected the spent cartridge and got another one into the chamber of the rifle at some point while the two were wrestling for the weapon. A second shot went off and it went through the lower portion of the entry door. At this point her boyfriend was successful in taking control of the rifle, getting it away from the suspect. He then ran from the residence, running to the neighbor's residence with the rifle in hand.

The female victim said, after her boyfriend ran out with the rifle, the suspect and her were arguing and he grabbed her and physically threw her across the room and against the cupboard. Her 2½ year old came out of the bedroom crying. She said she picked him up and took him back into his bedroom. She said she knew the suspect wouldn't hurt the children but she was afraid for her life. When she again exited the bedroom, the suspect was breaking everything in the house and she was in fear so she ran out and ran over to the neighbor's residence. She said the suspect was going crazy and she thought he was high on something. She had witnessed him angry before but he had never done anything like this, she said.

I told the female victim she should go before the court and request a temporary restraining order, (TRO). I suggested she contact women's services in Homer for assistance. I also told her the suspect would be in jail for a while but he did have a right to bail and, if he made bail, she should have the TRO in place so he'd know any contact would result in him again being locked up. She was given a domestic violence explanation card, which listed resources available to help her, as well as having all the contact telephone numbers, she would need.

Next, I contacted her boyfriend and conducted an interview with him, on record, and I tape recorded this conversation, as well. He said he had arrived at the residence shortly after midnight and they had watched television for a while and then had gone to bed. He said he slept near the wall and his girlfriend slept where she could easily exit the bed because of her two young boys sleeping in the other room. He said he was asleep when he heard a commotion and he looked up to see his girlfriend and the suspect fighting over the rifle. He said he heard the suspect say he would kill both of them. He told me he jumped out of bed and grabbed the rifle, and his girlfriend let go. He and the suspect continued to wrestle over the rifle and, at some point, the rifle fired, with the bullet going through the ceiling in the bedroom. He said the suspect was attempting to put another round in the weapon while he was trying to take the rifle away from him. They wrestled with one another down the hallway, ending up in the living room. He said he pushed the rifle into the suspect's chest and they went down onto the couch and turned the couch over, going over the back of it. The wrestling continued into the middle of the living room where they both were on the floor, fighting for control of the rifle, when it discharged a second time. This time he said the bullet hit the entry door.

Immediately following the second discharge, he said he was successful in taking the weapon from the suspect. He then ran out of the residence and over to the neighbor's residence, he said, to get the rifle where the suspect couldn't grab it again. He said he thought they were both going to die and he was very frightened. He said he and his girlfriend had been dating ever since the suspect and her had filed for divorce.

Following the interview, I collected the evidence we had gathered, and Officer Gruber and I returned to the police department. I logged the items into evidence and locked them in the evidence room. I then filled out the necessary paperwork needed to arraign the suspect. After that was completed, I called an airplane so I could fly the suspect to Homer and get him out of Seldovia. I felt it would be better to have him out of town, due to the close relationships both he and victims had in the community. Both of the male victims had been born and raised in Seldovia. At a time like this, everyone seems to think they have to take one side or the other. This can often cause problems which can usually be avoided by moving the suspect out of the area. I flew the suspect to Homer, where he was lodged in the Homer jail, and then then I returned to Seldovia.

I sent the necessary paperwork to the district attorney, and the lady, her boyfriend and I were all called to testify before the grand jury. We were told we could testify telephonically and I was sent subpoenas, which I served on the two victims.

The grand jury hearing was convened and the suspect was officially charged with two counts of assault with a deadly weapon. He could not be charged with criminal mischief for destroying the items in the residence, or for breaking out all the windows, because he was the owner of record and you cannot be charged with destroying you own property.

The suspect was held on a high bail but later pled no contest to one of the two charges and he was found guilty of one count of assault with a deadly weapon. The district attorney and the public defender reached a plea bargain, which is not unusual in this type of a case. The DA dismissed one of the charges for a no contest plea to one count of assault with a deadly weapon. The suspect received one year in jail with all but three months suspended, he was fined $1000 with $500 suspended, he was placed on probation for three years and ordered to have no contact with either of the victims. He was given permission to see his two boys under court appointed supervision.

The female victim did follow through and filled out the necessary application paperwork for a restraining order. The order was granted by the district court judge and the suspect was served with a copy of the order while he was in custody. (Case Closed by Arrest)

Note: *In domestic violence cases, no one really wins. It's a traumatic time for all involved but, in my opinion, the ones who suffer the most are the little ones. They don't' really understand what is going on and it can leave some long-lasting scars. Hopefully the two little ones, in this case, were able to get some counseling which, in my view, is vitally important. It had to be very frightening for them and they would need help dealing with the trauma.*

BURGLARY OF A DWELLING, THEFT IN THE SECOND DEGREE

It was around 0820 hours on the morning of November 6, 1989 when I received a call reporting an open door at the Joe Hayes residence, located in the east addition, the eastern part of town. Joe, his wife, Diane and I were best of friends, and I hated the thought of their house being broken into. Their house was empty most of the time and was always empty during the winter.

I quickly responded to the residence to check it out. When I arrived, I found the screen door to be wide open. Closer observation revealed the screen door, and the entry door to the mud porch, had both been forced open. The inner door, which had also been locked, had also been forced open, with damage clearly visible. I drew my weapon and slowly entered the residence.

The kitchen is the first room I would be going into and I observed moldy food, and dirty dishes, spread all around. The Hayes' kept a very tidy home, so there was no question about an intruder creating the mess. As I continued into the dining room, I observed dirty plates, with leftover food on them, sitting on the table. In the living room it was evident someone had been sleeping on the couch because a sleeping bag was lying on it and was spread open. No one was present in the resident but someone had been living there for, what appeared to be, a long period of time. Further perusal of the residence revealed a duffle bag, with cloths in it, and some mail addressed to a man who was now my prime suspect. As I checked the rest of the home, I found the door leading to the stairwell was also damaged and must have been locked prior to the suspect moving in. I walked upstairs but, not knowing what had been there, I had no idea what, if anything, was taken. I found evidence where a bath had been taken and a towel had been thrown on the floor. Soap and shampoo were on the sink and a can of Billy Beer was setting on the lid of the commode tank, opened and partially consumed. A razor and some shaving cream were also observed on the sink. Other than the area being used by the intruder, I found there was no damage in the upstairs part of the home. I went back downstairs and observed the sliding glass doors, leading to the outside deck area, on the west side of the structure, also had been damaged from the outside.

Apparently, the intruder had attempted to gain entry through the glass sliding doors and was unsuccessful. Considerable damage had occurred to the door frame with, what appeared to be, some type of pry bar.

After finding no one in the residence, I decided it would be a good time to take the needed photographs. I got my camera from the patrol vehicle and took a series of photographs of the damage, which was done, and of the personal property belonging to the intruder. After I had taken all the photographs, I started collecting evidence. I took anything which could have the intruder's fingerprints on it, including the dishes in the sink in the kitchen and on the table in the dining room. I took the duffle bag, with the intruder's belongings, and I took the items I'd found in the upstairs bathroom. After gathering all the evidence, I secured the home, as best I could, and I placed police crime scene tape across every entry. After I finished securing the residence, I returned to the police department. I tagged all the evidence and placed it in the evidence locker for later packaging for the crime laboratory.

I called Joe Hayes in Anchorage and told him about the forced entry to his residence and about all the personal items I found strewn around. He told me no one had permission to be in his house. He said the last time he was in Seldovia was in September when he winterized the residence. I told him about all the food and liquor which had been consumed and the mess that had been left by the intruder.

He told me he did keep food there as well as some liquor. I told him I'd keep him appraised of any progress in the case but I felt sure, with the evidence we had gathered, we would be bringing this before the court in a short period of time. He asked that I keep him appraised and we then ended our conversation.

As soon as I got off the phone with Mr. Hayes, I called the telephone company to ascertain what calls had been made within the last two months from the Haye's residence. I was told they could not be of any assistance until the middle of the month. They would not have that information until the 14th or 15th of November, they said.

My next call was to the electric company to find out if they could compare the electric bills for the last two months. They pulled up the information and a large discrepancy was found between September and October. From August 26th through September 26th the electricity used totaled $84.48 and, from September 26th through October 28th, a total of $311.84 in electricity was used, a difference of $227.36. It was evident the suspect had spent most all of October in the Hayes residence and had utilized the electric baseboard heaters for heating the residence.

Next, I went to the John Cabot cannery to find out if the suspect, whose name was on the mail I'd found, worked there. They said he had worked for them for a month and a half but had left and they heard he had gone to Homer to work on a fishing boat. I thanked them and returned to the police department. I called the harbor master in Homer and told him who I was looking for and asked if he knew him. He told me he didn't know him but he'd ask around and see if he could locate him. He said if the suspect was fishing on a boat out of his harbor, he should be pretty easy to locate. I told him not to alert the suspect that I was looking for him, if and when he found him, but to give me a call back. Two days later, at approximately 1345 hours, the Homer harbor master called me and said he'd located the suspect and he told me the name of the vessel he was fishing on. I thanked him and I called the Homer police department to see if they would assist me in the case. Sgt. Andy Klamser came on the phone and I gave him the information I had. He asked me to send him a fax with the facts of the case on it and he told me he'd pull the suspect in an interview him. I told him I'd fax him a report right away.

Officer Klamser did pick up the suspect and the man confessed to breaking into the Hayes' residence and staying there. He had broken in and had stayed there for over a month. He'd been working at the cannery and didn't have a place to stay so he'd broken into the Hayes' residence, ate their food and drank their alcohol, he told the officer. Following the interview, Officer Klamser arrested the suspect and charged him with burglary in the first degree and theft in the third degree, both felonies, and then booked him and locked him in a jail cell.

Like many of my cases, the man wound up pleading to the burglary and the theft was dismissed by the district attorney. He spent ten days in jail, had to pay restitution to Joe Hayes in the amount of $1642.34, which totaled the damages, the food eaten, the alcohol drank, plus the utility bills he had run up.

I was very pleased in that we were able to find the intruder rather quickly and the Hayes' family were compensated for the damage and the losses they would have had to absorb had he not been caught. I was also happy because I didn't have to pack up all the evidence I'd collected and send it to the AST lab. Of course, I was disappointed the district attorney wouldn't take the case at face value, but I was convinced that would never happen. We had all the evidence in the world, along with a confession, and it was a slam dunk case in my opinion. I still feel the DA's office treated cases in Seldovia differently than they did the cases they got from the police departments on the road system. I guess I need to be satisfied that the bad guy went to jail for a while anyway.

Joe and Diane Hayes have both passed on now, and I do miss them. I miss all our visits and I miss the stories we used to share. They were long time Alaskans and Joe was a State Legislator, Speaker of the House of Representatives for two terms and later, a lobbyist. He was a very pleasant man with a lot of history. I can honestly say I never met anyone who didn't like Dianne and Joe Hayes. They were two great people who I was proud to call friends. (Case Closed by Arrest)

1989, ANOTHER BUSY YEAR

1989 kept the police department busy with numerous investigations as well as responses to a number of calls for assistance. A total of 693 incidents were handled in 1989. The investigations which took place were a part of the 693 incidents. During 1989 we investigated three DWI's, served two arrest warrants, we had two vehicle accidents, one with injuries and we charged one person with criminal negligent burning. We charged one person with furnishing liquor to minors, investigated one report of damaging public property, investigated five assaults, charged one person with criminal mischief and one person was charged with driving without a license while two were charged with driving while license revoked. We had three assaults with deadly weapons, one physical assault, we charged one person with serving a drunken person on licensed premises, we dealt with two disorderly conduct calls, had one suspicious circumstance, wrote one citation for excessive speed, wrote one citation for negligent driving, dealt with one criminal trespass, investigated one death, investigated four burglaries of dwellings and we investigated three reports of theft. Given all the calls for assistance, we kept busy all year.

DOMESTIC VIOLENCE ASSAULT AND SAFE HOME PLACEMENT

I received an early morning call at approximately 0345 hrs. on January 7, 1990, from a concerned parent in Oregon. She had been in a conversation with her daughter, when the daughter's boyfriend terminated the call. The mother told me her daughter had called her when she was in a heated argument with her boyfriend and both of them had been drinking. The daughter told her mother the boyfriend had hit her and she was going to leave him. The caller was concerned for her daughter's, and her granddaughter's, safety and wanted the police to check on them. I assured her I would check on her daughter and granddaughter and told her I'd call her back with a report. I took her telephone number then called Officer John Gruber at his residence, telling him I would be picking him up to go with me. Any police officer knows it is not wise to respond to a domestic dispute alone.

I picked up Officer Gruber and we responded to the home where the domestic dispute was taking place. Upon stepping onto the porch, near the entry to the residence, yelling could be heard and it was very apparent there was a heated argument taking place inside. I knocked on the door and announced who we were and the male occupant yelled for us to come in. I attempted to open the door, but it was locked, and the man came and opened the door so we could enter. Upon our entering, the man asked what we wanted. I told him I had received a call from a person concerned about his girlfriend and her daughter's welfare. The man said everyone was fine and for us to leave his house. It was evident the man was intoxicated and very irritated. I told him we would not be leaving before I had contact with his girlfriend and her daughter. He said his girlfriend had locked herself in the bathroom, and if I wanted to see her, to go ahead and see if she would come out for us. It was at that time the lady unlocked the door and came out of the bathroom. It was readily apparent she, too, was intoxicated and very unsteady on her feet. She told us she'd locked herself in the bathroom because her boyfriend had hit her in the head with his fist and she ran into the bathroom to get away from him. The suspect denied hitting her and told us she had hit him in the face. Upon checking both subjects for an injury, I could find no evidence on either of them where they had been struck. Many times, injuries are not visible until later and this could very well be one of those times. However, to facilitate an arrest, I had to have evidence of an assault. The suspect said he wanted us out of his house and I told him we would leave after I conducted my investigation. He argued there was nothing to investigate. I asked the victim where her daughter was and she said she was staying with a friend for the night.

The suspect and the victim kept arguing back and forth and the suspect told me and Officer Gruber we didn't have a warrant and to get out of his home. He then jumped out of his chair in a challenging manner, and I pushed him back down in the chair with my right hand on his shoulder, and told him to sit there and not to approach me aggressively again or I would arrest him for disorderly conduct. The suspect continued his verbal assault on both Officer Gruber and I but didn't make any more aggressive actions. He told us to wait until Monday and he'd contact his attorney and he would take care of this. I told him he knew where to find me and I suggested he wait until Monday and let his attorney handle this or he could find himself locked up.

The victim told us she couldn't stay at the residence and I told her to get a few things together, she would be needing, and we'd see to her safety. She collected a few items and we escorted her from the residence. The suspect was still yelling at us when we exited the home.

He kept yelling that we would see what happened on Monday. Due to the lack of evidence, no arrest for a domestic assault could be made.

We went to the police department where I let the victim call her mother so her mother would know she and her daughter were safe. After she terminated the telephone conversation with her mother, I asked what had taken place at her home to start this fight. She said the suspect was at the bar and another man told him he'd heard he was whipping the victim's daughter and he had no business hitting the girl. The suspect had arrived home angry about being accosted by the man in the bar and this was what started the argument. She said the suspect hit her and she ran into the bathroom and locked the door to get away from him. When I asked what happened when she was talking to her mother on the phone, she said he was mad and he hung the phone up to keep her from talking to her mother. The victim told me she couldn't stay in Seldovia but she had no money and she didn't know what she was going to do. I advised her to get a temporary restraining order for protection and then I called the South Peninsula Women's Services office in Homer and left a message, asking that an advocate call who could talk with the victim regarding her next step. After a short time, a representative of South Peninsula Women's Services did call back and I gave the victim the phone. I then closed the door to my office and stepped out, so they could have a private conversation.

Following her talking to the advocate from women's services, I asked if she wanted to go to a safe home for the night. I told her, after she slept for a while, it would be easier to make any critical decisions she had to make. She agreed and told me she did need to sleep for a while. I called the safe home I utilized in these situations, and they told me to bring the victim to their residence. I took the victim to the safe home and asked that she not divulge to anyone where the safe home was located. She assured me she wouldn't tell anyone.

In this case no arrests were made and no charges were filed. Anytime an officer makes an arrest he/she must have evidence of a crime. In this case we had two intoxicated parties, each saying the other had assaulted them. We could find no bruising, bleeding, or any trauma visible to support their allegations. We did all we could do, given the circumstances. We separated the two for the night and seeing to the safety of both parties involved was all we could do to assist them. The victim did apply for a temporary restraining order and it was granted by the court but, as in most cases, the two did get back together and the TRO was recalled by the court upon the victim's request. Sometimes keeping people safe is all a police officer can do to assist in the domestic dispute. At least we did assist a person in a positive way. Without our involvement, the situation could have turned out quite differently. (Case Closed by Investigation)

A MATTER OF GUILT

On January 30, 1990 at approximately 1145 hours, I received one of the rarest of contacts I ever had. A man, who will refer to as Don, came to the police department and told me he wanted to talk to me about a number of criminal acts he had committed. He said, due to his religious beliefs, he needed to confess to a number of crimes. I started the tape recorder and I told him I'd like to first read him is Miranda warning and I read the rights to him. He signed the waiver of rights form and started telling me what all he'd been involved in. The crimes were fish & wildlife violations and he told me about one crime after another. Don said he had killed a goat, in both 1985 and 1986, using his wife's tags each time. He said he'd shot a seal in in November of 1989 and he shot an illegal bull moose on September 16, 1989. He said he took the bull moose with a .44 caliber pistol, while at the head of Jakolof Bay, near a lake. The moose's antlers measured thirty-eight inches, he said. Don continued telling me he had let a non-resident take a brown bear, on his tag, in the Post River area, on October 10, 1989, and he'd received $1000 in cash for this. He then admitted to taking up to fifteen king salmon, out of the Seldovia Slough, last summer and he knew he was only allowed two fish. He said he had also shot three ducks in January, 1990, knowing the season to be closed.

I told Don I would have to contact the Alaska Fish & Wildlife Agency and make them aware of the violations and they would most likely want to meet with him. He said he would talk to them anytime they wanted to meet with him. I told him I'd be in touch with him, but if he was going to leave the area, to let me know prior to going. He said he would not be going anywhere.

I called Trooper Bruce Bayes, who had transferred from a blue shirt trooper to a brown shirt trooper, and he made arrangements to come to Seldovia to talk to the suspect. (*Brown shirts are Alaska State Troopers who enforce fish and game laws, and dress in brown uniforms. Blue shirts are the Alaska State Troopers who dress in blue and regulate traffic and investigate criminal acts.*)

On February 2. 1990, at approximately 1330 hours, Don was again interviewed by myself and Fish & Wildlife Protection Officer, Bruce Bayes, and the conversation, like the first interview, was tape recorded. Trooper Bayes read Don his Miranda rights warning, a second time, and Don again signed another waiver of rights form. On this occasion he told us he'd shot two goats in the Red Mountain area in 1985 and then again in 1986. On both occasions he said he utilized both his tags and his wife's tags. He said on September 16, 1989, he'd shot a bull moose in the Jakolof Bay area near a lake, with his .44 caliber pistol. That moose's rack measured 38 inches and he said he knew it to be an illegal moose when he shot it. He said the rack was at a residence he had rented but would be hard to find in that it was buried in the deep snow. Don admitted he had also shot at a black bear, just prior to his taking the moose. He searched for the bear, he said, but was unable to find the bear or any blood. He said he must not have hit the bear but he felt he should report it. Don admitted he took a legal moose on his harvest ticket the same year, in the Post River area. He said the antlers on the legal moose measured 45 to 48 inches and they were at his residence, where he now lived. He said in 1988 he shot a seal and the meat was taken and eaten, and the hide was kept. He told us the hide is in the freezer at his residence. He said his wife was hoping for a seal coat one day. He admitted he had taken ten to fifteen king salmon in the summer of 1989 and he knew he was only allowed two fish. Don said, on October 10, 1989 he allowed a non-resident to take a brown bear on his tag and he received $1000 cash for doing so. He had fleshed the hide and salted it down and he then had the bear stamped by fish & game in Homer. He said he shipped the hide to a relative in Idaho to be delivered to a taxidermist. He told us the bear was a seven-foot, elderly sow. He also admitted he did not fill out an export tag, and he sent the hide by regular mail. He told us the man's name, who shot the bear, and where he lived in Idaho. The last thing he told us was he shot three ducks in January of 1990, knowing the season was closed. He said he had a dog and he was anxious to see him work.

Following the interview, Wildlife Trooper Bayes and I transported Don to his residence and confiscated a number of items, due to the illegal hunts. Taken were a .44 caliber pistol, 3 frozen ducks, moose antlers, (2 pieces), 1 frozen seal skin, 47 packages of moose burger, 12 packages of breakfast sausage, 9 packages of stew meat, 18 packages of round steak, 10 packages of moose back strap, 10 packages of ribs, 5 packages of tenderloin, 1 package of heart meat and 4 king salmon.

Wildlife Trooper Bayes informed Don he was under arrest and he would have to accompany him to Homer. I transported Trooper Bayes and Don, along with the confiscated items, to the airport where they boarded an airplane and flew to Homer.

At arraignment Don pled guilty to all the charges. He received a $5000 fine with $4000 suspended, 200 hours of Community Service, 200 days in jail with 170 days suspended, the 30 days in jail to start on November 1, 1990, his privilege to fish or hunt in the State was revoked for 2 years, he was placed on probation for 2 years and he was ordered to forfeit all the items we had collected at his residence.

This is the first case I've ever been involved in where the suspect came to the police department to confess to a number of different crimes he had committed. I do hope Don cleared his conscious and was at peace mentally, following his confessions. He left our area a number of years later, after he and his wife divorced. I must say I believe one's integrity defines who a person is, so, even though he committed a number of criminal acts, I have to admire the man for his honesty. He knew he would have to pay the price for his crimes before he ever came in and confessed. I sincerely hope Don was at peace after all of this was over. (Case Closed by Arrest)

Suicide Threat

On May 15, 1990, in the early morning hours at approximately 0217 hours, I received a call from the VPSO (Village Public Safety Officer) in Port Graham who told me about a local resident who was threatening suicide. I knew the man very well and knew he had a drinking problem. The VPSO said the man's brother was on the phone with their sister in the village. He told his sister he was with the man at a residence in Seldovia. The VPSO said the man was alleged to have a 30-30 caliber rifle pointed at his head and he was threatening to pull the trigger. They sister asked that the Seldovia police intervene.

I had a patrol officer at that time, who I will refer to as C-2. I called him and told him about the call and I told him I was responding and would meet him at the residence. I told him, if he arrived before I did, not to take any action and to wait until I arrived.

I got dressed quickly and put my police gear on then responded to the residence. C-2 had not arrived but I felt I could not wait. I had a very good relationship with the man and I felt I had a good chance of talking him down.

The man's wife met me at the door and told me not to come in. She said he'd told her if the police come in the door, he was going to pull the trigger. She had opened the door upon my arrival and I called out to the man, telling him who I was, and I asked if I could come in just to talk to him. He told me to stay away and he said he didn't want to talk to anyone. I could tell he was intoxicated by his slurred speech. I again told him I just wanted to talk and I felt we were good enough friends that he should not feel I was a threat. After a few minutes of talking back and forth, I felt it safe for me to enter the residence. I entered the kitchen/dining room area of the home and I saw him in a bedroom to the east of where I had entered. I could see him setting on the end of the bed with a 30-30 caliber rifle being held to his left temple area and his left hand was on the trigger. The rifle was in a fully cocked position. Having never been trained in this type negotiations, I played it by ear, taking a common sense approach. I asked if he would allow me to sit next to him so we could talk. He was hesitant to let me sit on the bed next to him so I entered the bedroom and stood beside the bed and continued to talk to him, trying to persuade him to give me the rifle.

The man's brother was setting in a chair on the north side of the bedroom and he seemed angry. He told me he could have handled this and the police weren't needed. I told him to be quiet and let me deal with the problem. He didn't say anything further and I continued my conversation with the man holding the rifle.

I told the man I was only there to help him and his family. His one-year old daughter was on the bed playing with a doll. I told him if he was to pull the trigger, he wouldn't be here to watch his little girl grow up and it would be very traumatic for her if he did shoot himself in front of her. He said she was too young to ever remember it and I disagreed and told him I didn't think so. I continued talking to him and I talked about him having a loving wife and the young daughter to think about. I asked him how they are going to continue on if he was to do this.

I heard C-2 drive up and I told the man's wife to have him wait outside the residence. She conveyed the message to him and he didn't enter the house.

I continued to talk to the man and over time I gained a good enough rapport with him, he finally allowed me to set down next to him on the end of the bed. I continued to talk to him, telling him his sister in Port Graham was so worried she had contacted the VPSO who, in turn, called me. I let him know he was impacting a lot of people and they would be crushed if he were to kill himself.

After I had taken a seat beside him, I devised a plan in my mind as to what I was going to do. I would keep him talking and I would wait, no matter how long it took, until the barrel of the weapon was removed from his temple area. I would then grab the barrel of the weapon with my left hand, making sure it was pointed in an upward direction where, if it did discharge, the round would go into the ceiling and not injure anyone. After grabbing the rifle with my left hand, I would grab the action with my right hand. If it did discharge, I would be holding it in a position where the bullet could only enter the ceiling area. Every minute felt like an hour and I kept talking to the man, telling him all the reasons he had to live. Our conversation continued for nearly forty-five minutes before the opportunity presented itself. He told me he was depressed because his mother had died and he should have died with her. He then became emotional and he moved the weapon a few inches away from his head. I grasped the opportunity and I grabbed the barrel of the rifle with my left hand, holding it so a round could only discharge into the ceiling. I then grabbed the action area of the cocked hammer with my right hand, preventing the hammer from coming down on the firing pin. I then pulled the rifle from his grasp. I immediately let the hammer down, insuring there would be no discharge. I handed the weapon to the man's brother and told him to give it to my patrol officer. He took the weapon and walked outside of the residence with it.

At this point the man was sobbing and apologizing to his wife. I was holding onto him, as someone would when hugging someone, which had a calming effect for him as well as giving me full control of his every action. His wife came over and he and his wife hugged for a time. As soon as he settled down, I told him he would have to come with me. I assured him, at this point he wasn't in any trouble, but I told him, he would have to get some counseling to avoid charges being filed. I told him he could be charged with misconduct involving weapons if he didn't follow through with the counseling and I assured him I would help him get set up with a counselor. I informed him it was also our policy to observe any suicidal victims until they were sober, and no longer a threat to themselves. He said he was no longer wanting to harm himself but I told him I would be putting him in jail for a few hours, until he sobered up. He seemed to accept this and I then told him we would have to go to Homer Mental Health, where he could get some assistance for whatever was bothering him.

The subject was transported to the Seldovia police department and was booked and locked in a jail cell. A jail guard was called and came in to guard the man. The guard was given strict directions regarding his guarding the suicidal victim. This entailed the guard observing the subject closely until he was no longer a suicide threat.

At 1100 hours, the following morning, I transported the man to Homer and turned him over to Homer Mental Health. He seemed grateful to be getting some help. He said he'd been depressed for a long time. I wished him the best of luck and I drove back to the airport, caught an airplane and returned to Seldovia.

It was nearly two years later when the man's 30-30 caliber rifle was returned to him. We still, to this day, remain friends. He did undergo counseling and had stopped drinking. I have not seen him in a few years, at this point, but everything I've heard has been positive. This incident could have been so much worse. I am so thankful it ended the way it did. (Case Closed by Referral to Homer Mental Health)

DWI - Driving Without a Driver's License - Criminal Mischief

On June 4, 1990, at approximately 2110 hours, a man flagged me down and reported he had just come from the airport and he had observed a man in a van, which belonged to Homer Air Serivce. He said he was starting it, flashing the lights and honking the horn. He stated he thought the man was intoxicated. I thanked him for the report and then responded to the Seldovia airport.

When I arrived at the airport, I observed a cloud of dust covering the airport apron area, and I further observed the Homer Air van to be in a different location than where it is normally kept. Skid marks and spin marks were visible on the airport apron and they had not been present on my last check of the airport only hours earlier. As I drove up to the van, a man exited the vehicle and I could tell he was very unsteady on his feet. I knew the man and when I contacted him, I asked if he had permission to drive the Homer Air van. He told me he did. I noticed he was having some difficulty in focusing and he had a strong odor of alcohol on his breath. His voice was badly slurred and his eyes were bloodshot. He said he always drives the van when he comes to Seldovia from his home in Port Graham. I asked if he'd had anything to drink and he said he'd drank two beers. I told him I needed to conduct a few sobriety tests to make sure he wasn't too intoxicated to drive. He told me he wasn't going to drive anymore so the tests weren't necessary. I told him to indulge me and I asked him to recite the American alphabet from the letter A to the letter Z. He said, "You mean the ABC's." I told him yes and to recite them, not to sing them. He attempted to recite the alphabet but could not finish on either of the two occasions he attempted the test. Next, I asked him to count backwards from ninety-seven to sixty-four. He counted backwards but, upon reaching ninety, he started back at ninety-seven again. I then asked him to do a balance test for me. I told him to lift his leg up off the ground in front of him approximately six inches and to hold it there until I counted to thirty. I showed him what was expected. He asked which leg and I told him he could use either leg. He attempted the test but kept putting his foot down on the ground to maintain his balance and I stopped the test in fear he'd fall. I then asked him to do the heel to toe test and I showed him what I expected. I told him to take seven steps forward, to turn around, and to take six steps back. He attempted the test and didn't touch his toe with his heel on one occasion and he stepped to the side two times to maintain his balance. He took more than seven steps before turning around and walking back to me and then he just walked back to where I was standing. I asked if he had an operator's license and he told me he didn't. I pulled my portable breath test instrument out of my vehicle and had him give me a sample of his breath. I was shocked to see a result of .355 blood alcohol content.

I advised the man he was under arrest for driving while intoxicated and for driving without a license. I would also be charging him with criminal mischief for the damage he had done to the apron of the airport. I placed him in handcuffs and set him in the front passenger seat of my patrol vehicle. I then checked for his personal items in the Homer Air van and I found nine, twelve packs of Miller Lite beer, in twelve oz. cans and one, twelve pack of Miller Lite beer with seven full twelve-ounce beers and two empty cans. I took all the alcohol as evidence.

I transported the man to the police department and read him his Miranda warning and he signed his waiver of rights form. He was interviewed and he admitted to driving the Homer Air's van without first obtaining permission and he admitted to spinning around on the airport apron. He further told me he didn't have an operator's license.

The necessary paperwork was filled out and the subject was given an Intoximeter breath test. The test resulted in a blood alcohol content of .287. Over an hour had passed since the subject had blown the .355 on the portable breath test instrument. After the subject made two phone calls to relatives in Port Graham, I booked him and locked him in a jail cell.

In preparing the case for arraignment, I called Homer police dispatch and did a background check on the subject. An arrest warrant was found for failure to satisfy judgement in a previous alcohol related case wherein the defendant hadn't followed through with his alcohol screening through South Kachemak Inc. Alcoholism Program, (SKIAP) as was court ordered.

I called a jail guard and he came in to guard the prisoner overnight.

At approximately 1030 hrs. the following morning, I showed the defendant his rights film and then called Homer court. The subject was arraigned telephonically on charges of driving while intoxicated, driving without a license and criminally mischief. The judge was further made aware of the bench warrant. The defendant requested an attorney and the judge automatically entered a not guilty plea. The judge asked questions relating to the defendant's finances and a public defender was appointed to his case. Bail was set and a $1000 unsecured bond was signed. He was ordered not to consume alcohol and not to leave the third judicial district without first obtaining permission from the court.

At the court's calendar call for the case, the district attorney and the public defender had reached a plea agreement wherein if the defendant pled guilty to the driving while intoxicated, the other charges would be dismissed. The defendant pled guilty to the driving while intoxicated charge and was fined $500 with $250 suspended, he was ordered to serve thirty days in jail with twenty-seven suspended and he was to turn himself in at the Seldovia jail on June 7, 1990, at 1300 hours. He was placed on probation for one year and he was admonished for not having followed up with SKIAP and he was ordered to go to S KIAP today, following his being sentenced and he was again ordered to comply with their recommendations. He was told to refrain from consuming alcohol and he was placed on probation for one year. He was also told his privilege to apply for an operator's license was revoked for a period of ninety days.

The subject failed to turn himself in to serve his three days on the driving while intoxicated charge and I had to request an arrest warrant through the court so he would be forced to serve the sentence. He was arrested the following week in Port Graham, by the Alaska State Troopers, and he served his three days in jail at the Seldovia jail. (Case Closed by Arrest)

DWI Suspect, Nearly Release

On June 14, 1990, at approximately 1820 hours, I received a citizen complaint reporting a man driving a maroon and gray pickup truck on Rocky Road in an erratic manner. The caller said the truck was loaded with garbage and it was blowing out, all over the road, and he thought the driver was intoxicated. He said the man was most likely going to the landfill, to get rid of the garbage, but he felt it should be covered with something so it wouldn't blow all over. I assured the man we'd look into it and thanked him for the call.

My patrol officer, who I'll refer to as C-2, was on duty so I called him on the radio and told him about the complaint and further told him to respond and to let me know what he found. I had no sooner finished my radio conversation with C-2 when a fire call came in, reporting a fire at the landfill. I usually respond with the fire department so I geared up and left my residence in route to the landfill. I was on Rocky Road, on the straight stretch, where I observed C-2 had the maroon and gray pickup pulled over. I slowly passed them and I observed C-2 and the driver to be standing by the driver's door of the pickup. The man was holding onto the door, possibly to maintain his balance, and I could see he was having difficulty in focusing. I thought the man was highly intoxicated by my limited observations just in passing. I expected to receive a call from C-2 telling me he had the man in custody and that I would be needed at the police department for an intoximeter test, since C-2 was not certified on the instrument.

As I continued on past the two, I called C-2 on the radio to see if he needed any assistance. He assured me he had it handled so I continued on to the landfill. When I arrived, the fire department had responded and they were hosing down a trash fire that had gotten started. I stood by in case I was needed.

After waiting long enough for C-2 to conduct the necessary tests for driving while intoxicated, I called him on the radio for a status report. He told me the driver was only borderline DWI and he would just give him a ride home. Because of my suspicions, I told C-2 I wanted to see the man and I directed him to bring the suspect to the landfill. He said he would be underway and I waited for them to arrive. When they did arrive, C-2 walked up to my window and I asked him if he'd put the man through field sobriety tests. He said he had and the man was borderline and probably could be taken for DWI but he thought it would be best if he just took him home. I said, "Well I want to talk to him first."

I exited my vehicle and walked back to C-2's patrol vehicle and asked the man to step out. I noticed he was very unsteady on his feet when he exited and I told him I wanted to put him through some field sobriety tests. He told me C-2 had already put him through some tests. His speech was slurred and his eyes were bloodshot. He smelled strongly of alcohol and, as stated, he was unstable on his feet. I asked him to recite the alphabet from A through Z and he said he couldn't recite it backwards. I told him to just recite it forward from A through Z. He attempted to recite it but failed. He tried a second time but each time he failed to continue and he got some of the letters out of sequence. When he was asked to count backwards, he also failed. I found a flat spot and showed him how I wanted him to do the heel to toe test and when he attempted this test, he kept stepping to the side to keep from falling. I told him we were stopping the field sobriety tests before he hurt himself. I pulled out my portable breath test (PBT) instrument and had him give me a breath sample. He blew a .350 blood alcohol and I told him he was under arrest for driving while intoxicated. I placed him in handcuffs and put him in the passenger seat of my patrol vehicle. I told C-2 I would transport the suspect to

the police department and for him to get the necessary vehicle information we would need and to secure the man's vehicle. Another man,
also intoxicated, was sitting in the back seat of C-2's vehicle and I told
C-2 to deliver the man where ever he was going and I'd meet him at
the police department.

To say I was upset with C-2 would be a gross understatement. We
had been butting heads for a while now and I had recently reprimanded
him for the way he was doing his bar checks. C-2 was on nights for
most all of his shifts, and I was told he would spend most of his shift
in the bars, visiting with all the patrons. I had three separate complaints from different people stating he was spending too much time
in the bars. I told him, when I first found out about it, he was to take
a walk through the bars every couple of hours to see if there were any
problems, but he was not to stay in the bars visiting with everyone.
I put in writing the procedure I wanted followed, so he would not
misunderstand what I required, and he could not say, down the road,
I hadn't discussed it with him. C-2 told me he had his own way of
doing bar checks and it had worked for him for many years in other
police departments. I told him he wasn't working for other police departments now, and as long as he was working for me, he'd do the bar
checks in the manner which I had explained to him. After his telling
me the suspect was borderline DWI, I felt he was dishonest with me
and it made me wonder if he would ever initiate an arrest on anyone
from the bars. He was pretty much one of the bar crowd himself, and
that's not acceptable when policing a small community.

The suspect was transported to the police department and he was
interviewed after receiving his Miranda warning and signing his waiver
of rights form. He admitted to drinking 4 beers and said he was on
his way to the landfill to unload the garbage in his vehicle. Following
the interview, and the filing out of all the necessary paperwork, the
suspect submitted to an Intoximeter test. The test resulted in a blood
alcohol content of .247. The Intoximeter test was given approximately
one hour after the portable breath test, which had resulted in a .350
blood alcohol content reading. This is a very high breath alcohol and,
to think, C-2 had described him as borderline and was going to take

him home and release him. This kept eating at me. After the suspect was placed in a cell, I told C-2 we would need to have a talk the next day but I was so angry at the present time, I might say some things I shouldn't. I told C-2 to be in my office the next day at the start of his shift. He said he'd be there. I told him he could go back on patrol and I'd handle the paperwork and get this case ready for the courts. C-2 left the office and I went to work on the paperwork.

I did a background check on the suspect, through the Homer police dispatch. Dispatcher, Greg McCullough informed me there was a warrant outstanding on my suspect out of the Soldotna office of the Alaska State Troopers. He said the warrant was for failure to satisfy the alcohol screening requirement on a previous DWI arrest. He also said bail was set at $150.00 on the warrant. He'd found the subject's operator's license was in a state of revocation and the man was subsequently charged with driving while license revoked. Bail was set at $1,150.00 cash, $500.00 each for the two misdemeanors and the $150.00 bail for the warrant. His step-father called inquiring about the bail and I informed him of the amount. In approximately one-half hour the man's step-father came to the police department with $1,150.00 in cash and the suspect was released after signing a promise to appear for arraignment on June 31, 1990 at 1330 hours at the Seldovia police department. He would be arraigned telephonically from my office. The release form also restricted him from consuming any alcoholic beverages or entering any establishment whose main purpose was the sale of alcohol. I advised him, if he violated the conditions of release, he could be arrested and charged with another crime.

On June 25, 1990, at approximately 0820 hours I arrived at the police department to continue doing the paperwork for the DWI/DWLR case. When I entered my office, I found an envelope addressed to me lying on my desk, along with C-2's radio, his keys to the vehicle, the office keys and the keys to the city complex.

When I opened the envelope, I found a resignation letter signed by C-2. He wrote that the working relationship he was accustomed to, in previous police departments, was not occurring in the Seldovia police department and he felt I was close minded and would not listen to his side of things. He said he had worked in numerous police departments, and was the chief of police in a few of them, and he said he has never been treated the way I had treated him. He said, due to our unfortunate differences, he was giving his notice of his last day of work to be two weeks from this date. The letter continued stating, because he had accumulated sufficient vacation time to cover the next two weeks, he would be taking his leave immediately, two weeks prior to the date his resignation was effective. He said he was saddened we could not work together but this should be taken as a lesson by me and I should have some schooling in the handling of subordinates.

I called the city manager and told him about the letter of resignation and the manager told me C-2 had also given them a letter. He said the letter said some pretty disparaging things about me as a chief of police. I told the manager we had different philosophy's and I found C-2 to be less than truthful in his dealings. I also told him I felt I couldn't have continued working with him after an incident that had occurred the previous day, anyway. I also told the manager I would bring a copy of the letter of resignation he wrote me and I would fill him in on what has been happening in the department. I made a copy of the letter and then responded to the city manager's office. I gave him the copy and shared with him what had taken place on the DWI stop. I didn't leave anything out and I told the city manager, anyone working with me, in the police department, better know they have to do their job honestly and above board. I filled him in regarding the reprimand I had given C-2 relating to the way he did bar checks. I explained to him that a police officer is not supposed to remain in the bars most of his shift and buddy up to the patrons. I said this was something C-2 did not agree with. I also informed him I would have been coming to him today to discuss terminating C-2 had he not given his resignation. The city manager told me to go back to work and we would see how this all shook out. I thanked him for listening and left his office.

The suspect pled guilty to DWI and was sentenced to a $5,000 fine with $4,000 suspended and he was ordered to 360 in jail with 300 days suspended. He was also ordered to comply with the recommendations of South Kachemak Inc. Alcohol Program (SKIAP) and he was ordered to have no criminal violations for five years. The defendant also pled guilty of driving while license revoked (DWLR) and was fined $5,000 with $4,000 suspended, to run consecutively with the DWI sentence. He was also ordered to serve 180 days in jail with 80 days suspended, and 30 of the jail sentence may be served in an in-house alcohol/drug program. His operator license was revoked for 10 years, to run consecutively with his DWI sentencing. He was also ordered to comply with recommendations of SKIAP, which again is to run consecutively with the DWI sentencing. He was further placed on probation for 5 years.

The defendant had an extensive criminal record and his sentencing reflected that fact. He would hopefully get the help he needed and would take advantage of the in-house alcohol/drug option the judge gave him. (Case Closed by Arrest)

DISGRUNTLED EMPLOYEE

On the morning of July 1, 1990, I received a call from the city manager and was told my patrol officer, the same police officer as in the previous story, C-2, was requesting a meeting with the city council concerning an employee issue. He was said to have a list of things he wanted to share with the council concerning the police department and the way it was being managed. The city manager said the meeting was scheduled for 1930 hours on July 3, 1990, at the multi-purpose room. I thanked the manager and told him I'd be there.

I wasn't concerned all that much regarding the upcoming meeting because I hadn't crossed any boundaries I shouldn't have crossed. I always conducted my business up front and honestly. In my view, this was no more than an attempt by C-2 to hopefully convince the council he would make a better chief of police than I. I have no doubt he saw the writing on the wall, regarding his continued employment, after the way he botched the DWI case. I'm convinced this is why he gave his resignation when he did. I had previously written him up for hanging out in the bars and buddying up to the patrons instead of policing the bars, and he was clearly upset about that. As a result, I warned him I wouldn't let him get away with selective enforcement. I firmly believed he would never arrest, or bring charges against, any of his bar friends. Life would be a lot easier at times if we could pick and choose who we charged but that wasn't going to happen as long as I was chief of police.

I arrived at the council chambers a few minutes before the meeting was to start. C-2 had given his resignation, and in my view, was no longer employed by the city. Because the meeting was held in an executive session, I cannot divulge what was said, however, I can tell you C-2 had twelve different items in writing he brought before council, which were very defamatory towards me. Prior to the meeting getting underway, I was given a copy of the allegations and, following C-2's presentation, I was given the opportunity to answer each and every allegation. I answered each allegation and I also brought out a few more incidents C-2 had avoided bringing up. I pointed out some false statements and some exaggerated statements C-2 had made and I explained my feelings on everything else C-2 had brought before them. To make a long story short, I told the council I would continue to run the police department with integrity and professionalism, the same way I had *been running it*. I also told them I would not tolerate any subordinate of mine to work dishonestly and, if that was what was expected, then they should certainly find another chief of police. I explained to the Council, if a police officer was found to be dishonest, it painted a dark picture off the entire police department.

When the council re-convened to an open meeting, the matter was not mentioned and no action was taken. I was later told by three of the six council members, they were more than happy with my performance. They could have ordered the manager to terminate me but that didn't happen and I stuck around another twenty plus years. C-2, after not being successful in his coup attempt, felt he had no future in Seldovia and he moved back to wherever he came from. He was not a happy man the last time I saw him but I noticed he did seem to spend considerably more time in the bars prior to leaving our fair city. My ears should have been ringing, I have no doubt.

Following the meeting I thought back to what my father had taught me from the time I can first remember his sharing his philosophy with me. He said, if a man is honest in his dealings, when times get tough, or if he is ever challenged regarding his endeavors, he will always be exonerated. He said when a man is honest, he does not have to worry about his actions, they are most always in his memory bank. He also told me, if I were honest in all my dealings, it will be noticed and I would build a reputation of honesty and, because of this, many doors will be opened for me. A man of good character never wants for a job, he said. He told all his sons, if we can be trusted, we would go far in this world. By taking my father's advice, honesty did pay off, and I've witnessed this time and again. I've had a lot of opportunities made available and many doors have been opened for me. I will continue to go through life always endeavoring to be as honest as possible and attempt to live up to the standards my father taught me.

Theft 3rd Degree and DWI Watercraft

On June 20, 1990, at approximately 1720 hours, I received a call from the village public safety officer (VPSO) in Port Graham reporting a man from their village had stolen a white skiff, with a fifty horsepower Johnson outboard on it, and he had reportedly headed for Seldovia. The VPSO said the suspect had been drinking prior to leaving the village but he didn't know if he was intoxicated. He said the man didn't have permission from the owner to use the skiff.

I called my patrol officer, who will refer to as C-4, and told him about the call and directed him to take up a position on the city dock and to alert me by radio when he observed a white skiff coming into the bay.

Approximately fifty minutes later C-4 reported he had the skiff in sight and it was headed for the small boat harbor. I responded and observed the skiff enter the harbor between the breakwaters. The suspect landed at the launch ramp and nosed the boat up to it. He shut the engine off and then exited the boat, tying it up to a rock nearby. When he walked up the ramp, I observed him to stagger somewhat and to be unsteady on his feet. I met him at the top of the ramp. I knew him personally and he told me hello and said it was good to see me. I thought to myself, his being glad to see me was about to change.

I asked the suspect if he had permission to use the skiff. He told me he had been using the skiff around Port Graham for the last three months. I informed him I'd received a call stating he'd taken the skiff

106

without permission. He said he had been using the skiff all along and didn't think he needed to ask permission. His speech was slurred and I smelled alcohol on his breath. I told him I wanted to put him through a few tests to make sure he wasn't too intoxicated to legally operate the skiff. It was apparent to me he was not happy about this but he went along with it and attempted to do the tests I requested of him. He couldn't recite the American alphabet without leaving out some letters and, when counting backwards, he got to a certain number then he started over again. I asked he perform a heel to toe test for me and I showed him what was expected. At this point he said, "Hell Andy, you know I'm drunk. Just arrest me." At that point I placed him in handcuffs and told him he was under arrest for driving a watercraft while intoxicated, and possibly, for theft in the third degree, for taking the skiff without permission. He again told me he had been using the skiff for months now.

I told C-4 to take the skiff over to the float and tie it up and to bring the gas tank, the hose, and any other valuables, up to the office to insure no one else took them. I told him I'd pick him up and transport him back to his patrol vehicle. When C-4 did come up from securing the skiff, he had two rod and reels and a rifle which he'd taken, along with the gas tank and hose.

Upon reaching the police department with the suspect, I read him his Miranda warning and he refused to be interviewed, stating I knew he was drunk. He did submit to an Intoximeter breath test which resulted in a reading of a .173 blood alcohol. That is over two times the legal limit to be operating a motor vehicle. Following the Intoximeter examination, the suspect was fingerprinted, his mug shots were taken and he was locked in the jail cell. He was told bail would be $500, cash only. He told me he couldn't make bail. A jail guard was called and came in to watch over the prisoner. An alternate jailer was called to relieve the original guard after his eight-hour shift.

After the suspect was arrested, I called the VPSO again, and told him to check to see if the owner of the skiff wanted to pursue the theft charges for the suspect taking the skiff. I told the VPSO what the suspect told me about his using the skiff for the last three months. The VPSO called me back and told me the owner of the skiff was just happy to get his skiff back, and since the suspect was being charged for driving it while he was drunk, he didn't think it was necessary to charge him with theft. The VPSO said the skiff owner was making arrangements to come after his skiff. I told the officer to tell the owner we had his gas tank at the police department and we would give it to him when he came to pick up the boat.

On June 21, 1990, at approximately 1100 hours the suspect was telephonically arraigned on charges of DWI watercraft and he pled no contest to the charge. Judge Engle found him guilty but set the sentencing off until June 28, 1990. An unsecured bond of $500 was ordered, the suspect was told to abstain from consuming alcoholic beverages, not to enter any bar or businesses whose main income was derived from the sale of alcoholic beverages, and not to leave the third judicial district without permission of the court. He was further ordered to break no laws.

On June 28, 1990 the subject was sentenced to 60 days in jail with 30 days suspended, he was fined $750.00 with $450.00 suspended, he was ordered to comply with the recommendation of SKIAP and, to abstain from drinking any alcohol. He was placed on probation for two years.

Another successful case out of the way. I'm just glad we were able to stop the suspect from picking up more alcohol and heading back to Port Graham, as intoxicated as he was. His reason for traveling to Seldovia in the first place, was to obtain more alcohol. Anything could have happened had he continued to drink and head back to the village in the skiff. (Case Closed by Arrest)

NOTE: *The sentencing in this case was put over until a later date so the subject's criminal record could be viewed to ascertain the contents of his criminal past. Upon finding that he did have an extensive criminal record, the judge sentenced him to a greater length of time in jail and a higher fine than would normally be the case. The defendant's criminal record showed numerous listings of alcohol related crimes.*

As stated, I was acquainted with the defendant and we had a good relationship. We were not close friends, but back in my fishing days, we had met and had gotten acquainted. He was a good man but alcohol had taken over his life and he did things he wouldn't normally do, when sober. I felt bad for him and hoped he would get the help he needed.

DWI, Expired Registration, Refuse Portable Breath Test

I t was December 24th, 1990, at approximately 1640 hours when I observed a green Pontiac sedan leave the Post Office area heading west on Main Street. The driver caught my attention when he was spinning out and fishtailing right in front of me. I was somewhat surprised because I thought he had to have seen me. I was in my marked patrol vehicle, at the intersection by the post office and I felt it odd this had occurred. I followed the vehicle and observed him swerve in the left-hand lane when going around the corner just below the old Lutheran Church. The driver then made an abrupt left turn into the parking lot at the store and parked his vehicle. I pulled into the parking lot and pulled up on the west side of his car. As soon as I parked the man exited his vehicle and started walking away in an easterly direction. I called out to him and told him I wanted to talk to him. He asked what about and I told him it was about his erratic driving. I asked why he had spun out and fishtailed on Main Street when leaving the Post Office area. He responded, stating he was having some problems with his accelerator sticking at times. I walked over to him and asked if he'd been drinking any alcohol today. When I got close to him, I smelled alcohol on his breath. He denied drinking but when I told him I smelled alcohol on him, he admitted to having two beers. (*It seems whenever a driver admits to drinking it is always only two beers.*) I told the subject, due to his erratic driving and the smell of alcohol on his breath, I was going to have to put him through a series of field sobriety tests. He became irritated and stated he wasn't drunk and this was just police harassment. I told him to appease me and I started the tests.

The first test was the standard balance tests wherein I asked the subject to stand with his arms at his sides, to life one leg approximately six inches off the ground and to hold it in that position until I counted to 30. I then showed him what was expected. He lifted his left foot off the ground approximately six inches and attempted to hold that position but was unable to do so, putting it down on three separate occasions, to keep from falling. I stopped the test fearing he might fall. I then asked that he recite the American alphabet from the letter "A" to the letter "Z." He attempted this but left out some letters. The next test was the heel to toe test. He was instructed to take seven steps forward, to turn around and to take six steps back. He was further instructed to count out loud each step and to touch his toe of his foot with the heel of his other foot on each step. Again, I demonstrated what was expected. He took a number of steps forward without counting or touching his toe with his heel on most of the steps. He turned around and walked back to me without touching his toe with the heel of his other foot at all. He also took eleven steps before stopping. The last test was the counting test and I asked that he count from eighty-six backwards to sixty-five. On his first attempt he counted backwards to eighty without any errors but then jumped to sixty-nine and kept counting until he reached sixty. I then retrieved the portable breath test instrument from the patrol car and asked that he give me a breath sample. He refused, stating he wasn't going to blow on that thing and he further stated I had to watch him for fifteen minutes before he had to blow. I told him if he refused to blow, he would be receiving a citation. He still refused telling me he knew his rights. I never argued with him, and I told him to turn around and informed him he was under arrest for driving while intoxicated.

I transported the man to the police department and we went through the booking process. I read him his Miranda rights warning and I filled out the necessary paperwork. He refused to sign the waiver of rights form. He was then given the right to an independent blood test and he refused. He was observed for approximately thirty minutes, ensuring he had nothing in his mouth, prior to his being asked to provide a breath sample on the

Intoximeter. He provided a breath sample which resulted in a finding of a .166 blood alcohol content. As mandated by law, I also administratively revoked his driver's license and gave him a temporary seven-day license. I retained his driver's license so it could be sent in to the State of Alaska.

Following the booking process I called Magistrate Coughenower in the Homer Court and she ordered the subject be released on his own recognizance, following his signing a promise to appear form and agree to the conditions that he appear for arraignment, not consume any alcohol or go into any establishment whose main business is the sale of alcohol. He had to also agree to obey all laws and ordinances. He signed his paperwork and I released him as directed by the Magistrate.

At arraignment the subject pled no contest and he was fined $500.00 with $250.00 suspended, he was sentenced to thirty days in jail with twenty-seven days suspended, his operator license was revoked for ninety days, concurrent with the administrative revocation, and he was placed on probation for one year. (Case closed by arrest)

NOTE: *This case was not so different from any other case, wherein a subject is arrested for driving while intoxicated, but I felt the need to write about this one because it was a difficult case for me. I knew who the driver was when I observed his erratic driving, and I knew there would be some hard feelings for any actions I would take following the investigation. You see the subject was a relative on my wife's side. It would have been so easy for me to have ignored what I'd seen and just keep driving down Main Street, but I took an oath which meant I'd enforce the laws regardless of who it was who violated them. During my tenure I had many occasions wherein I was dealing with relatives on my wife's side of the family. I'm sure if I'd had any relatives on my side, living in the area, I would have also been dealing with them on occasion. My actions did have an impact and my immediate family felt it more during the holidays. Our social lives got to be less and less. It is part of policing a small area where you or your spouse was born and raised. I'm not making any excuses, nor am I offering any apologizes for doing my job. I'm only trying to emphasize some of the difficulties which comes with policing a small area where nearly everyone is known by the police officer.*

1990, a Busy Year

During the year of 1990 we had a total of six hundred and eighteen incidents. The investigations conducted during 1990 consisted of one physical assault, two domestic violence assaults, one Alaska Fish and Wildlife case, two burgles of a dwelling cases, two child abuse cases, one case of criminal trespass, one death investigation, one credit card theft, one property theft case, two automobile accidents, two criminal mischief cases, two disorderly conduct cases, one attempted suicide case, two driving watercraft while intoxicated cases, four driving while intoxicated cases, one case of refusing breath test instrument, one driving with license revoked case, three driving without a license cases, one furnishing liquor to minors case, one case of failure to satisfy judgement, one welfare of infant case, one welfare check case, one civil disturbance case and one vehicle with expired registration case. With everything else going on, we kept quite busy given the daily patrols and the never-ending paperwork that accompanies all investigations and/or any actions taken by a police officer.

ASSAULT WITH A DEADLY WEAPON

On February 2, 1991, at approximately 0010 hours, I was awakened by a call from a lady on the east side of town, commonly referred to as the East Addition, telling me a man had just been to her door requesting police respond to his residence. She said he had reportedly been stabbed in the shoulder with a knife. I asked the caller if the bleeding was controlled and she said she really didn't know. She said he was only at her door for a minute and asked that she call the police.

After receiving the call, I contacted officer John Gruber and told him about the call and told him I would be picking him up at his residence. I then called the EMT's and asked that they respond to the resident in question reference a knife wound. I informed the EMT dispatch, the EMTs should obtain clearance before they entered the residence upon arrival. I then responded to Gruber's residence running with overhead lights but no siren. (Commonly known as running code-2.) Officer Gruber joined me and we responded to the residence in the East Addition. We reached the residence at approximately 0022 hours and I activated my pocket cassette recorder to record any upcoming statements. The EMTs were yet to arrive.

When Officer Gruber and I entered the residence, I observed the male victim setting in a recliner while his girlfriend, the suspect, was setting on the edge of a hide-a-bed, next to him. A young boy and girl were setting by the suspect. The victim was not wearing a T-shirt and a knife wound was visible on the inside upper right arm, near the armpit. The bleeding was controlled, however there was evidence of blood on, and around the wound. Further observation revealed a number of scratches on his chest and arms.

The female suspect had her hands tied behind her back and blood was visible on her shirt. She was clad only in a dark T-shirt and panties. She smelled of alcohol and when she spoke her voice was slurred. She asked me to untie her. I told her I would release her but if there were any problems, I would put her in handcuffs. She assured me there would be no problems. At that point I cut her restraints and I observed blood on her arms and on her hands. I asked the suspect if she was injured in any way and she told me her right shoulder was hurting her.

I asked Officer Gruber to get the camera from the patrol vehicle. I then asked the victim what had happened. He told me he had to restrain his girlfriend because she was going to break all the windows out of the home. He said she was angry because he would not go to the bar and get her more alcohol.

The EMTs arrived on scene and, via radio, asked for clearance to enter the residence. Clearance was given and the EMTs came in to treat the victim. I asked that the EMTs wait until I could photograph the wound, the scratches and the blood on the victim before they treated him. After I finished photographing the victim the EMTs treated him and then called EMT dispatch to have them alert Doctor Reynolds they would be transporting the victim to the clinic and he would need to be treated by the doctor. Dispatch called the EMTs back, after a time, and told them the doctor would meet him at the clinic.

As I looked around the home, I observed a can of Budweiser beer to be setting on the table in the kitchen area. The beer can was found to be less than half full. Further observations of the home revealed four more empty beer cans in the garbage in the kitchen area. Blood was visible on the floor in the kitchen and a black handled filet knife was observed laying on the floor by the trash can. Blood was also visible on the black plastic handle of the knife. I took photographs of the kitchen area, the filet knife, the blood on the floor and all the beer cans, both in the garbage can and the one on the table. These items were tagged, bagged and taken as evidence.

The EMTs finished their examination of the victim and prepared him for transport. The suspect complained of shoulder pain and this information was relayed to the EMTs. An EMT checked the suspect but told me she could not help her, other than put the arm in a sling and the suspect did not want that to happen. The EMT told her she would see if the doctor could look at the suspect's shoulder. The victim was ambulatory and was able to walk to the ambulance and did not have to be placed on a stretcher.

I asked Officer Gruber to transport the two children to the clinic in the patrol car so they would be out of the residence when I affected the arrest on their mother. I continued to investigate the scene while Officer Gruber transported the two youngsters to the clinic. I suggested the suspect put her pants on and get her jacket and shoes and told her she was going to have to come to the police department. Officer Gruber returned shortly and I placed the suspect in handcuffs and told her she was under arrest for assault in the second degree. Officer Gruber and I then transported the suspect to the Seldovia Police Department.

Upon arrival at the police department I read the Miranda warning to the suspect and, upon her signing the waiver of rights form, I interviewed her. The interview was tape recorded.

The suspect stated she had consumed five beers but had not drank any other alcohol. She further stated she was the only one drinking and the victim had not consumed any alcohol. She stated she had started consuming alcohol at approximately 8:00 PM and the argument, and subsequent fight, occurred at approximately 11:30 PM. She said she had told the victim she was going to leave and go back to Anchorage to her husband. She said he threatened he would tie her up to keep her from leaving. She told me she entered the kitchen area while they were still arguing and she retrieved the filet knife from behind the dishes in the sink. She said he then entered the kitchen area and she was holding the knife, telling him to stay back. She said he charged her and ran onto the knife. At the same time, she said she jabbed forward with the knife and he wound up getting stabbed in the shoulder. After he had been stabbed, he grabbed her and threw her to the floor, holding her arms behind her back. She said he yelled for her son to get him a belt or something so he could tie her up. When no help came, he dragged her into the bedroom where he found a shoelace which he used to tie her arms behind her back. The victim allowed her to walk around the house after she was bound. She said he then yelled for her son to go call the police. Since there was no phone in the house, and the boy was afraid to go out in the dark, the victim went to the neighbor's house himself and asked that they call the police.

The suspect was still complaining of her right shoulder hurting so I called the clinic and talked with Doctor Reynolds. The doctor told me he would come to the police department and examine her shoulder as soon as he finished with the victim.

The doctor did respond to the police department and did examine the suspect's shoulder, but said he could not do anything further without first taking x-rays. The suspect told him she did not want to have x-rays taken. The doctor, prior to leaving the police department, told me if there were any other problems to give him a call. He said if she was still having problems in the morning to let him know and he would x-ray the shoulder.

A female jail guard was called to guard the prisoner overnight and the suspect was booked and placed in the jail cell. Since the charge was a felony, she would have to post $5000 cash to bail out. This, of course, was not going to happen.

At approximately 0145 hrs., 2/21/91, the victim was interviewed at the Seldovia police department. The interview was tape recorded.

The victim told me the suspect had started drinking beer at around 9:00 PM and she was consuming her beer rather quickly. He said he noticed she was starting to get irritated and more violent. She told the victim she wanted more alcohol and asked him to go to the bar and get her more beer. He said, when he refused, she told him she would break every window out of the house. He said she entered the kitchen area, where he thought she was going after a pot or something which she would use to break the windows. He said he went into the kitchen area to stop her from breaking the windows and she pulled a filet knife out of the kitchen drawer. The victim said he told her to put it down but she took a couple swipes at him, trying to cut him. He said he was unsure what to do but thought if he could get control of her arm, he could control the knife. He said he lunged forward to grab her arm at the same time she jabbed out with the knife, stabbing him in the shoulder. He said, after being stabbed, he wrestled her to the floor, getting the knife away from her and pinning her arms behind her back. He said he yelled for the suspect's son to him to get him a belt or something he could tie the suspect up with. After there was no response by the suspect's son, he said he dragged the suspect into the bedroom where he was able to locate a shoestring which he used to tie her hands behind her back. He then took her back into the living room area and ask the boy to go call the police. The suspect's son, being afraid to go out that time of the night, refused and the victim decided he would contact the neighbors and have them call the police. He said after going to the neighbor and requesting they call the police, he returned home and nothing more had occurred before the police arrived. The victim said the whole reason for tying the suspect up was to keep her from breaking the windows out of the home, not to keep her from returning to Anchorage to her husband.

In the afternoon of the 2/21/91, at approximately 1535 hrs., I interviewed the eight-year-old son of the suspect. Jan Wyland, counselor for Homer Mental Health, was asked to set in on the interview in hopes it would make the youngster feel more comfortable.

The youngster told me he was awakened by his mother and the victim yelling at one another. He said the victim had called for him to get a belt or something so his mother could be tied up. The boy said he did not get a belt for the victim. He said his mother had been drinking beer and she and the victim had gotten into an argument. All of the yelling had awakened he and his sister. The boy stated he was aware his mother had stabbed the victim and he had observed blood on the kitchen floor and on the rug but he had not seen the actual assault. He had observed the stab wound on the victim's shoulder and the blood on the victim chest and arms. He did see the victim dragging his mother into the bedroom where she was tied up with shoelaces.

At approximately 1554 hours, 2/21/91, I interviewed the nine-year-old daughter of the suspect with Jan Wyland being present during the interview. The girl told us she and her brother had been awakened by the yelling and arguing between her mother and the victim. She said the victim was yelling for her brother to get a belt or something to tie her mother up so her mother could not hurt any of them. She said her mother had been drinking beer. She said she was not aware of the victim having any alcohol at all. After being awakened she observed her mother being dragged into the bedroom by the victim when he was attempting to find something to tie her up. He was able to locate a shoelace and use that to tie her mother's hands behind her back. She told me when the victim went to the neighbors to call the police, her mother had asked her to untie her hands but the victim had returned before she could attempt to do so. She said she did not see the assault take place but she had observed the blood on the floor in the kitchen and on the rug in the living room. She had also observed the wound in the victim's shoulder and the blood on his arms and chest.

After the investigation was complete, I determined that an argument had ensued between boyfriend and girlfriend, primarily due to alcohol consumption. The suspect, because her boyfriend would not go to the bar and get her more alcohol, had grabbed a knife in the kitchen and had taken two swipes at him, trying to cut him. In an attempt to get the knife, the victim had lunged toward the suspect at the same time she had jabbed forward with the weapon wherein the victim sustained a stab wound to his upper right arm just below the armpit. The suspect was arrested and charged with assault in the 3rd degree, a C class felony. The suspect was held overnight and then transported to the Homer jail.

The court system failed to send a disposition of this case and I never did find out the sentencing guidelines. The family moved from Seldovia shortly after the incidents and I have never seen them since. (Case closed by arrest)

AUTOMOBILE ACCIDENT

At approximately 1703 hours, 3/18/91, I was notified of a two-car vehicle accident which had occurred on the Jakolof Bay Road, at approximately 2.5 mile. The person reporting the accident did not know if there were any injuries because he did not talk to those involved, but it appeared there were no serious injuries, because everyone was standing around talking. Two other vehicles were also parked in the area; possibly concerned citizen who stopped to help.

Directly following the report, a lady, whom we will call Jane, called stating she had been involved in the accident. She told me she was calling from her residence after getting a ride home from a friend. She said she would be returning to the scene of the accident. When asked if any injuries had been sustained, she stated she had cut her right knee and she had hit the windshield with her head with such force it had broken the windshield. She stated she did not need the EMT's, and would be seeking medical assistance after a time, if she felt it was warranted.

I responded to the scene of the accident and upon arrival I saw Jane's vehicle pointed in a northerly direction and it was in a ditch on the west side of the road. The vehicle was up on a snow berm and it appeared it had been pushed backwards, ending up where it now set. I observed considerable damage to the front of the vehicle. The windshield on the driver's side was broken and skid marks indicated the vehicle had been pushed backward from the center of the roadway into the snow berm, with the skid marks being approximately forty to fifty feet long. It was evident by the marks on the roadway that Jane had attempted to avoid a collision with the oncoming vehicle. Lying directly in front of Jane's vehicle was a yellow snowplow, which I later discovered had been broken off the other involved vehicle, upon impact. Other debris was strewn around in front of Jane's vehicle which included a broken part off the grill and a silver cooking pot.

A man, who we will call Jerry, was driving the pickup that collided with Jane's vehicle. He had a snowplow attached to the front of his vehicle when the accident occurred. His vehicle was now parked on the west side of the roadway approximately twenty-five to thirty feet north of Jane's vehicle. His vehicle was facing in a southerly direction.

I inquired of Jerry if anyone had been injured, other than Jane, and he stated he did not think so, and said his family was fine. He stated no one was complaining of any injury other than Jane. He didn't feel Jane was seriously injured as she was walking around and had gotten a ride to her residence. Jerry said his wife and two children were in his vehicle at the time of the collision. Jerry 's vehicle, along with the snowplow being broken off, had the grill damage but the hydraulic pump and plow attachments were still in place and did not appear to be damaged.

Jane returned to the scene of the accident and when I questioned her, she told me she had been headed home, in a northerly direction, following a vehicle being driven by a man we will call Joe. A vehicle coming toward them, traveling in a southerly direction, was being driven by a man we will call Peter. When Peter passed Joe, a cooking pot fell out of the back of his vehicle. Alice stated Joe stopped his vehicle on the roadway to pick up the cooking pot. Being stopped in her lane of traffic, Jane realized she was traveling too fast and did not have time to stop without colliding with Joe's vehicle. To avoid a collision with Joe's vehicle, she attempted to pass and steered into the oncoming lane of traffic. As soon as she started around Joe's vehicle, she observed Jerry's vehicle approaching. Jane told me she tried to stop and avoid the accident, but was unable to. She stated she estimated her speed at 25 mile per hour. Jane stated she was not wearing a seatbelt at the time.

Due to her sustaining injuries in the accident, I suggested Jane seek medical help from Doctor Reynolds at the Seldovia clinic. I told her when a head injury occurs it is always good to seek professional assistance. She agreed and I arranged transportation for her to the Seldovia clinic.

Jane later reported that she had sustained no lasting injuries, and other than being bruised and knocked around, she would be fine. Prior to her being taken to the clinic I had obtained her operator's license, registration and insurance information.

When I approached Jerry, he produced his driver's license and registration but told me he did not have any insurance. He told me he was headed in a southerly direction, into town, when he had observed Joe's vehicle stopped on the roadway in the oncoming lane of traffic. He said he then saw Jane's vehicle starting to pass Joe, in his lane. Jerry estimated his speed between 20 and 25 mile per hour. He said he attempted to stop but could not avoid the collision. Because his vehicle was much heavier than Jane's vehicle, she was pushed backwards into the snow berm. He stated, to open the roadway for traffic, he backed his vehicle to where it now sat. Jerry said his wife had hit the dashboard upon impact but she was not in need of medical attention.

I approached Joe, who had remained at the scene of the accident, and asked for his operator license, registration and insurance information. After he produced the needed documentation, I asked him to tell me what had happened from his perspective.

Joe said he was traveling in a northerly direction, going home, and he had observed Jane following behind him back approximately five or six car lengths. He said he saw Peter was approaching him and when Peter passed him, he observed a cooking pot fall out of the back of Peter's vehicle. Joe said he then observed Jerry coming toward him, and he thought he would stop, get the pot, flag Jerry down, and give it to him so he could deliver it to Peter. Joe stated after he stopped his vehicle, Jane had attempted to pass him and collided with Jerry. He said he did not understand how Jane did not see his brake lights when he stopped. Joe told the officer he was wearing his seatbelt and he really did not feel that he contributed to the accident. He felt Jane should have been able to stop behind him and let Jerry pass.

After everyone had been interviewed at the scene, the snowplow was loaded into the back of Jerry's pickup truck and Jane's vehicle was towed to her house.

The following day I got word to Jane that I wanted to re-interview her, and ask if she could come by the Seldovia police department. When she arrived, I asked her if she would mind outlining the accident again for me on record. She agreed and told me she had been following behind the vehicle driven by Joe, and when they met Peter, she had observed Peter swerve pretty close to Joe, nearly causing a collision between the two of them. She stated she had then watched Peter closely when he had passed her, due to his nearly hitting Joe. She stated as soon as Peter had passed her, she observed Joe to be stopped in the roadway. She said she was traveling too fast to stop in time so she attempted to go around Joe's vehicle. She then observed Jerry's vehicle coming toward her and, although she tried to avoid the accident, she could not.

Following the second interview with Jane, I called Peter and ask if he would come to the police department where I could interview him. He stated he could be in within an hour. Upon his arrival I interviewed him on record and ask if he had witnessed the accident. He stated he had not witnessed the accident but had been told about it. He said he was told it happened right after he had passed Jane. I asked him if he had lost a cooking pot from the back of his vehicle. Peter said he was not aware of any cooking pot in his vehicle but was told that one had fallen out on the roadway. He said he did not remember ever having a cooking pot in his truck. He estimated Jane's and Joe's speed between thirty-five and forty mile per hour. I thanked Peter and we ended the interview.

After the investigation was complete, I found there were a number of violations which needed to be addressed. A number of factors came into play which, in my opinion, contributed to the accident. First the pot calling out of the back of Peter's vehicle started the chain of events. Because of this Peter was cited for failure to contain and confine a load. Secondly, Jane was cited for basic speed, for driving too fast for conditions, and failure to wear a seatbelt. Thirdly, Joe was cited for stopping, standing or parking on a roadway, and lastly, Jerry and his wife were cited for failure to wear their seatbelts and for failing to have vehicle insurance. This concluded the investigation of the accident. (Case closed by investigation)

NOTE: *In my opinion, it would have been unfair if citations were not written for each violation, regardless of who was responsible. I have always tried to conduct my investigations without any bias or favoritism at all. I cannot over emphasize the importance of conducting each investigation by making one's decisions based strictly on the evidence obtained and one should never make decisions based on relationships or who might be involved. If you desire longevity in policing a small area, this is one of the major factors you will have to consider. You will find on many occasions it would be so easy to cite a person you do not care for and let someone you like slide but, that would be dishonest, and honesty is by far the most important factor for obtaining longevity.*

First-Degree Murder/ First-Degree Robbery

I t was Friday, 3/22/91, at approximately 5:20 PM, when I received a call from Alaska State Trooper, John Adams. Trooper Adams was with judicial services at the time, and was responsible for prisoner transports around the state, as well as ensuring prisoners arrived for their court hearings on time. On this occasion, Trooper Adams had delivered a prisoner to the Homer jail facility and was calling from the Homer AST post. The Alaska State Troopers and Homer Police Department shared the building and both utilized the dispatchers, who were hired by the Homer Police Department.

Trooper Adams told me they had a situation under way and could possibly use my assistance. He first asked if I had a police scanner and when I told him I did not, he told me there was somebody, who we'll refer to as David, who was talking to a girlfriend in one of the Russian villages. Trooper Adams said David told his girlfriend he had killed his father. The entire conversation was being transmitted through some device where it could be scanned. An Alaska State Trooper, who overheard the transmission, activated his pocket voice recorder and recorded the entire conversation. Both the Alaska State Troopers and Homer Police Department personnel were trying to identify the caller, to ascertain the location, but had not been able to do so. Trooper Adams said the caller told his girlfriend he had knocked on the door and when his father opened it, he shot him through the chest with a high-powered rifle. The caller also told his girlfriend his father was so fat they had to wrap the wire around him and drag him out of the building when they were going to dispose of the body. The caller added they had to put a plastic bag over his father's head and chest area, due to the excessive bleeding.

At one point the girlfriend had mentioned a man, who we will call Joe, when referring to David's father. With this information I suspected the call to be coming from the home of some people I knew who lived outside of Seldovia in a remote area. I told Trooper Adams, if this was who I thought it was, Joe had been in my office two weeks prior to this and was complaining about David being on drugs and stealing money from him and his wife. Joe told me his wife was working out of Dutch Harbor on a foreign vessel, as an observer, but, when she came back to town, they were going to prosecute David for theft. He said this was not the first time this had happened. I told trooper Adams I thought I knew the people involved and I was asked if the Seldovia Police Department would respond to the area to check and see if this was the location they were trying to identify, as well as find out if there was, in fact, a homicide.

I called my patrol officer, who we will refer to as C-3, and told him about the call and informed him we would be responding to Joe's residence and for him to wear his bulletproof vest and bring his rifle. I also would be wearing my vest and would be taking a shotgun, along with my duty weapon. *(Rarely did we wear a bulletproof vest when going about our duties in our small department. I have been chastised by other police officers for not wearing the vest. However, the life threatening, violent crimes were not abundant in our area.)*

Because there were no roads to the residence, I had to call on a friend, at the Kasistna Bay Laboratory, and ask if he would take us from Jakolof Harbor to an area near Joe's residence. He said he would meet us at the harbor and he would have his skiff ready to go when we arrived. As soon as we had the gear we needed, C-3 and I responded in my police vehicle.

We arrived at the Jakolof Harbor and boarded the skiff. We left Jakolof Bay and were transported to the beach, approximately 300 yards to the north of Joe's residence. Due to the circumstances, we avoided landing on the beach where we were visible from the residence. The area between Joe's house and where we landed on the beach, had only long grass and tree stumps. The area had been logged off, clear-cut, with all the trees removed. There was approximately 8 to 10 inches of snow on the ground and walking was not difficult. I decided we would approach the residence from two sides. I sent C-3 around the beach and I proceeded across the logged off area. Even though we were not sure we were at the right location, we had to proceed with caution, as if a crime had occurred and the suspect was still in the area. There was very little cover as I approached the residence and I felt very vulnerable. C-3, walking around the beach, was able to approach the scene by staying low and using the tall grass as a cover, most of the way. Me, being 6'3" tall, with a heavy build, didn't find the stumps to be very comforting. As we approached the building, I observed tracks from a four-wheeler and also observed blood on the ground near where the north entrance to the steps on the deck was located. After C-3 and I reached the location, I walked up the steps and onto the deck, coming in from the north, while C-3 came up the steps on the south side of the deck. We observed drag marks across the deck, along with droplets of blood. The snow had melted off the deck but the drag marks were very prominent. When I saw the drag marks, I thought about what David had said about dragging his father across the deck. After I reached the entry door, I motioned for C-3 to approach and to take up a position on the opposite side of the door. I observed considerably more blood on the threshold outside the door and I tried the door to see if it was unlocked. Finding it unlocked, I nodded to C-3 and swung the door open wide. There was no movement inside but, just inside the doorway was pools of blood on the floor. It appeared someone had tried to clean it up but had only managed to smear it around. I told C-3 to cover me and I made entry. I told him to wait at the entrance, so as not to destroy any more evidence than possible. There was a wall to the right upon entry and it continued three quarters of the way into the room. I stepped around the blood and continued inside the structure to see if there was anyone present. When I reached the end of the partition, I looked around the corner and found no one there. I checked the rest of the residence and, finding no one, we proceeded to search the area outside.

I remember the adrenaline rush, and the fear, that accompanied it. It was evident we had found the crime scene and, even more evident, was the fact that someone had been injured, and possibly killed. With the information we had at this time, with all the blood, we were convinced we would be finding a body. In a small-town police department this type of crime doesn't occur on a regular basis. Even though you'd been trained in conducting searches, searching for suspects and evidence retention, we didn't get a lot of practice in that respect, thank goodness.

I exited the residence and we proceeded to do a search of the area and the other buildings. We wanted to determine if David was still at the location. We again observed the four-wheeler tracks to be very prominent in the area and, the more we followed the tracks, the more blood we found. There were two other outbuildings, one being an A-frame and the other a storage shed. We cleared both buildings and were pretty sure David was no longer at this location. We would still be vigilant, not knowing of all the places a person could hide.

Feeling pretty confident we were alone at the residence, C-3 and I started following the four-wheeler tracks. One set of tracks led to the north, into the clear-cut area. As we followed the tracks, more blood became visible. We stayed off the main track to avoid destroying any evidence and walked on either side of the four-wheeler tracks. Approximately eighty yards into the clear-cut area, we found a wooden box. The box measured approximately 4-foot-wide by 4-foot-long, by 4 foot-high. It was a square box made of wood with those dimensions. Upon closer observation we found the top of the box was not covered. As we approached the box, I observed wooden sticks, grass and some clothing, partially covering a body. Closer observation revealed someone had attempted to start a fire but were not successful. Some of the clothing was charred but the fire went out before it ignited the wood. The body had been placed in the box, face down with his feet nearly reaching the top of the box. There were no shoes on the man's feet but he still had socks on. Due to evidentiary reasons, I did not want to disturb the box or the remains. It was evident there was nothing we could do to save the man's life at this point, so all we could do was protect the evidence.

I called Homer police dispatch on my radio and told them we had a 10-79, code for a deceased person. Dispatch informed the Alaska State Troopers and, via radio, the trooper asked if I could find a landline telephone so we could discuss some details which would be needed for a search warrant. I told him the only telephone in the area was the one the suspect had used when he had been monitored. I also told the trooper I had no way to get on the road system without a skiff. It was decided I would make the call over the radio/telephone in the residence, while being careful not to destroy any evidence or say anything that we didn't want made public.

C-3 and I walked back to the crime scene and, while he waited outside and kept watch, I entered the building to make the phone call. Being evidence conscious, I was very careful in my entry into the building. The telephone was located on the east wall of the building near the table. As I approached the telephone I observed, what appeared to be, a bullet hole, just above, and to the left of the window, on the east wall. I would make the troopers aware of this when they came to collect evidence.

I wrapped my handkerchief around the receiver of the phone before using it. After making contact with the trooper, I described the crime scene, the building I was in, the outbuildings and the general area. This information would be needed for the search warrant affidavit. I was asked by the trooper to stay on scene and keep the area secure until troopers could arrive to gather evidence and pick up the body. It was getting late in the day and it appeared it would be the next morning before the troopers could fly in with the helicopter. We would have to make ourselves as comfortable as we could outside the residence and make sure nobody approached the area.

The telephone, which was used by David and myself, is known as a radio/telephone. It interconnects with the telephone system through radio transmissions. Because the signal comes from a radio transmission to a landline on the Homer Spit, any conversations from the phone could be scanned. David most likely was not aware of this because, had he known, I'm sure he would not have said many of the things he told his girlfriend.

I conveyed to C-3 what had been requested of us and we made ourselves as comfortable as possible, outside the residence. We hadn't brought any food or water with us and I hadn't eaten dinner when the call came in so, as you can imagine, it made for a long night. The temperature in March was still in the upper 20's and we hadn't planned to spend the night. At least it wasn't snowing or blowing so it could've been a lot worse.

It was around 9:30 PM when we were laid-back, waiting for morning to come, when a rifle shot rang out. When you are not expecting something like this it's hard to determine what direction the noise came from. We quickly took cover, not knowing if we were the targets, and then we observed a vehicle on the Jakolof Road turn its lights on and speed away. By now, there was no doubt the rumors were flying, and someone thought it would be funny to shoot a rifle in the area. It's hard to describe the feelings one has at a time like this, not knowing what next was going to happen, but nothing more occurred during the night. I radioed Homer police dispatch and told them of someone shooting before we knew where the shot had come from. After we were convinced the shot came from, I again called Homer police dispatch and conveyed what we had observed to them.

Homer police dispatch has always been the dispatch for emergencies in, and around, Seldovia. Since 1981, when we negotiated a contract with the Department of Public Safety, the Homer police dispatch has taken us under their wings and treated us as one of their own. In times like this, knowing our wives would be worried about us, dispatch would call them every few hours, reassuring them that we were safe and not in harm's way. Any time we responded to any call, which lasted longer than planned, the dispatchers would call and reassure our wives we were fine and that the case was taking longer than planned.

It was a long and miserable night but the next morning the sun came up just after 9:00 AM and it lifted our spirits somewhat. At approximately 9:45 AM the Alaska State Troopers arrived via helicopter. Corporal Dan Weatherly exited the aircraft and he had brought three other people with him. Andy Klamser, a Homer police officer, took all the photographs when we were collecting evidence. One of the other officers kept a running log of the evidence and the photographs. The Alaska State Troopers are very thorough when they do a crime scene and it took a number of hours. Joe's body was removed from the wooden box and I observed a garbage bag had been placed over his head and reached to his waist, as per the suspects statement to his girlfriend. Wire had been wrapped around his upper torso and coincided with the statement he had made, as well. The bullet hole had gone completely through Joe's body and it was found lodged in the east wall just to the left of the window, where I had observed what appeared to be a bullet hole. After all the evidence was gathered, Joe's body was placed in a body bag and was loaded on the helicopter. Corporal Weatherly accompanied the body, and the evidence to Homer. The helicopter then returned and picked up the other equipment, the officers had brought with them, and the other three officers were flown back to Homer, as well. I contacted my friend at the Kasistna Bay Lab, and he provided transportation for C-3 and me back to the Jakolof Bay Harbor.

The Alaska State Troopers were the leads in the case and I only wrote up a supplement report. The district attorney, Sharon Isley, traveled to Seldovia, via the trooper helicopter, and picked me up before going to the crime scene. Everyone else was busy and they needed the logistics, so I was asked to go along. Ms. Isley and her associate took pictures and took notes. They questioned two or three people who lived in the area and then delivered me back to Seldovia.

David, and an associate, had been observed walking into the Homer airport area following their return to Homer, after leaving the crime scene. They had launched a skiff from the crime scene, and had taken it to the Homer Harbor. They then caught a ride up the spit to the airport. After they had walked into the airport, the police lost track of them and later found they had exited in a vehicle. Two days later the trooper's arrested David, his girlfriend and her brother. A lot of information came out during the interviews. The interviews revealed the crime was pre-meditated. David, his girlfriend and her brother had set around the table planning what they would do. David would come to Seldovia, with his girlfriend's brother, and they would catch a ride out to the area. David and his girlfriend brother would walk in and David would go to the building, where they kept the firearms, and would get a rifle. He would then go to where his father would be working and he would shoot him. The investigation showed David and his girlfriend's brother did exactly as they had planned. The motive was robbery. David wanted the checkbooks and other records, and he took these before leaving the area. With the checkbook and other records David could extract money from the family's account.

I did not get a copy of the disposition in this case but I was told David was sentenced to sixty-two years behind bars after being charged with First-Degree Robbery and First-Degree Murder. I was also told this is the first case, on the Kenai Peninsula, where a guilty plea was made, with no plea-bargaining, in a First-Degree Murder/First-Degree Robbery case. With the telephone conversation having been recorded as evidence, it would be hard to deny what was stated during that call.

In police slang, these type cases are known as a *SLAM DUNK*. (Case Closed by Agency Assist)

NOTE: *This case was one of the most impacting cases of my nearly 32-year career. I was acquainted with all those involved, with the exception of the girlfriend's brother. I'd had two previous police related cases involving David, and we weren't on the best of terms. I hadn't seen David for a couple years but had stayed in contact with his father, his mother and sister. I was told David and his father had a very rocky relationship for many years. In a case of this magnitude, there are many victims. It's sad how many people were negatively impacted. Hopefully, for those of you who have the belief nothing of significance ever happens criminally in small areas, this should change your mind. Crime is not determined by the number of people who live in an area, but what's in the people's hearts and minds. Police seem to always arrive after the fact, to pick up the pieces, and are rarely there to stop the event. In this instance, the perpetrators only wanted to obtain money so they could continue to supply drugs for their addiction.*

ASSAULT 2ND DEGREE/MISCONDUCT INVOLVING A CONTROLLED SUBSTANCE

On 3/30/91, at approximately 2300 hours, while my patrol officer, who I will refer to as C-3, and I were at the police department, we received a phone call from the Linwood Bar reporting a fight in progress and they said the police were needed right away. Both C-3 and I responded in separate vehicles. When I entered, I observed a large group of people restraining two individuals, who had apparently been in the fight. Upon approaching the crowd, I observed both men, who were being restrained, had blood on their face from some open wounds.

I immediately, via radio, called the EMTs, requesting they respond to the bar. C-3 and I broke up the crowd and started putting together what had actually occurred. C-3 questioned one of the individuals involved while I questioned the other. I talked to Jerry, one of the men in the previous case, and he stated the other man, who we will call Larry, came to Seldovia on a tugboat. Jerry said he had seen Larry earlier at the Seldovia Lodge but he did not know the man. Larry was creating problems with everyone at the Lodge so Jerry said he left and came to the Linwood. It was not long until Larry showed up at the Linwood and continued his harassment of everyone. Jerry said Larry sat down at the bar and there was one empty barstool between them. Jerry continued by saying they got into a verbal argument and Larry hit him in the side of his head with a bar glass, cutting him. He said at that point, the fight was on. Jerry told me he took Larry to the floor and they were both wrestling and swinging at one another until they were pulled apart by the onlookers. Larry was complaining that he had a broken back, Jerry said, but he would not stay down, even though the crowd tried to keep him there. Jerry was adamant that he wanted to press charges of assault against Larry.

It was apparent Jerry had been drinking but his speech was not slurred and he carried on a conversation without any problem and he was not unsteady on his feet. Even though he had been consuming alcohol, I concluded he was not impaired.

The EMTs arrived on scene and treated both subjects. Larry was still complaining about having a broken back, but he would not follow any EMT instructions. He had lacerations on the side of his face and a cut across the bridge of his nose. After some discussion, he finally did let the EMTs clean and bandage his wounds. He still refused to let the EMTs transport him to the Seldovia clinic for further examination by Doctor Reynolds.

C-3, who was first to contact Larry, relayed to me that Larry was complaining he had a broken back, when he first contacted him. C-3 said Larry would not stay on the floor, even though he was told not to move. When he refused to stay down, C-3 had him set on a barstool at the bar and asked an EMT to check him out. Larry was combative, verbally abusive to the police and the EMTs, as well as everyone around him, and he refused any medical attention by the EMTs.

Other patrons were interviewed on scene and everyone agreed Larry had started the argument and three of the patrons we talked to, observed him hit Jerry in the face with the bar glass. There was glass fragments and blood on the floor where the two had been fighting. Larry was not forthcoming as to what had taken place and only cursed C-3, threatening to kill him and myself, and everyone else in the bar.

I questioned the bartender and he told me Larry came into the bar in an intoxicated state and ordered a drink. He said he refused him service at first but he was so abusive and repeatedly threatened to get him fired so, to shut him up, he poured a small splash of whiskey into a glass of Coke and gave it to him. I informed the bartender, in these type cases, we were only a telephone call anyway. The bartender said immediately following his serving him, Larry started being very verbally abusive toward Jerry. There was one empty barstool between the two and Larry kept poking at Jerry with his hand. Jerry turned around and told him to stop and put his arm up to block Larry's hand when he attempted to poke him again. It was at that time Larry hit Jerry in the side of the face with a bar glass, cutting his face and forehead. He said Jerry then grabbed Larry, after he was hit with a glass, and took him to the floor. They wrestled and punched one another until broken up by the crowd. It was at that time when the police entered the bar, the bartender stated.

After interviewing the bartender, I informed Larry he was under arrest for assault in the third degree. I then turned him around and pushed him into the bar and placed him in handcuffs. A pat down search of his person revealed a small baggie of vegetable matter, which appeared to be marijuana, in his right front pocket. The vegetable matter and the fragments of broken glass on the floor, with blood visible on them, were taken as evidence.

I transported Larry to the Seldovia clinic where I met with Doctor Larry Reynolds. Because Larry was complaining of having a broken back, it was imperative that he be examined by Doctor Reynolds, before being lodged in the Seldovia jail. Even though he was verbally abusive and arrogant, Doctor Reynolds was able to check his wounds, bandage them and release him to me for incarceration. Doctor Reynolds informed me he could find nothing indicating an injury to Larry's back but told me if there were any further complications, to call him.

I transported the suspect to the Seldovia police department where I thoroughly searched his pockets and then booked him into jail on charges of assault in the second degree. After placing him in the cell, I took the vegetable matter, which was taken off his person, and checked it with a NIK kit. It tested positive for the presence of THC, the hallucinogenic that is found in marijuana. Larry was subsequently charged with another misdemeanor count of misconduct involving a controlled substance in the sixth degree.

C-3 had been assisting EMTs and was still on scene, still conducting the investigation. Upon his arrival at the police department he shared what had occurred when he first had contact with Larry. He stated Larry was setting on the floor and there was blood and glass beside him. Larry told the officer he struck Jerry with the bar glass because he had a broken back and Jerry was threatening him. He said Jerry was bigger than him and he was only defending himself. C-3, fearing he could have a back injury, said he tried to keep Jerry in a stationary position, but Larry would not stay sitting down. The officer said Larry was very descriptive in how he hit Jerry with the glass, using his hand to show the officer how he hit and twisted the glass upon impact.

I did not do a formal interview with Larry, due to his degree of intoxication. Ever since our first contact with him he had been verbally abusive and uncooperative. He had repeatedly threatened to kill both C-3 and myself and there was no reasoning with him. I could see no reason to even attempt a formal interview with him due to all the corroborating evidence we already had. Everyone present in the bar, at the time of the incident, was in agreement as to what had taken place. If he wanted to give a statement, I would read him his Miranda warning in the morning and conduct a formal interview.

Larry was incarcerated overnight in the Seldovia jail and was arraigned telephonically at 10:30 AM the next morning. He pled not guilty on both the assault charge and the marijuana charge. Due to his financial status a public defender was assigned to his case. On 6/11/91 Larry went before the Homer court, on a change of plea hearing, and pled no contest to a lesser charge of disorderly conduct. The district attorney and Larry's attorney had come to an agreement and the felony assault charge was reduced to disorderly conduct, so a violation is what he pled to. Larry received a $1000 fine with $500 suspended, he was given credit for one day served in jail and he was placed on probation for one year.

On the charges of misconduct involving a controlled substance in the sixth degree, Larry pled no contest, as well. He was fined $500 with $250 suspended, was placed on probation for one year, which was to run consecutive with his previous probationary order, and he

135

was ordered to undergo alcohol and substance abuse screening by June 21st. (Case closed by arrest)

NOTE: *Even though Larry had an extensive criminal background, the two attorneys got together and decided to lessen the charge of assault, a C class felony, to disorderly conduct, a violation, which guarantees no jail time would be served. Had the assault in the third degree held up, Larry would most probably have had to serve possibly sixty days in jail, with a criminal background such as his. It bothered me when the felony assault was reduced to a violation, when it could've been reduced to a misdemeanor assault. A misdemeanor assault, with Larry's criminal record, would most probably have ensured some jail time. It has been my findings, over the years, the district attorney's office has failed the Seldovia area repeatedly, by either reducing our dismissing charges brought by the Seldovia Police Department. This is not something new and still seems to be going on today. I understand they are very busy with a heavy caseload but it is my feeling justice is not being served in the Seldovia area on most cases. I've come to the conclusion, because it costs more to try a case from Seldovia, they tend to dismiss, or lesson, any serious charges we file with them.*

HARASSMENT

On 4/3/91, at approximately 1104 hours I received a call from Homer police dispatch. The dispatcher stated they had received a complaint from one of their local residents, who stated he was being harassed by someone from Seldovia. Repeated telephone calls over the last week to ten days had been made to the complainant's home phone. On most occasions the caller would just click the receiver off and on but would never say anything but, on one occasion, the caller left a message on the complainant's phone recorder.

The dispatcher stated a line trap had been placed on the complainant's telephone and they had been able to identify the telephone number from where the calls originated. The complainant stated he had listened to the voice recording but could not identify the caller by his voice.

I asked the dispatcher if she could play the message for me so I could record it on my pocket recorder. She played the message and I recorded it. I did not recognize the voice of the person making the call, either. I was given the Homer police department's case number and I told the dispatcher I would look into it and get back to them.

Even though we had the telephone number, we were not sure where the telephone was located. I contacted the telephone company and they gave me the location as being a pay phone at the Susan B. English school. Having the voice recording with me, I responded to the Susan B. English school at approximately 1500 hrs., where I met with Mike

Smith, the principal of the school. The complainant had written down
the time and date when the obscene call had been made. He gained
that information from his telephone recorder. I informed Mister Smith
what had taken place, giving him the date and time, the recorded call
was made. I also played the voice recording for Mister Smith and he
stated he did not recognize the person's voice. He said there had been
a volleyball/basketball tournament over the weekend in question, and
the tournament coincided with the timeframe when the recorded call
had been made. A number of harassing phone calls were made on a
Saturday, which was the same day the message was left on the complainant's telephone recorder.

The principal and I discussed which students would be most likely
to make harassing phone calls and we came up with four possibilities.
We then prioritized them, listing the ones more likely to have been
involved. We then listed persons who hung out with our suspects. We
prioritized who we would first interview, picking a student who would
most likely be truthful with us and, if they had any knowledge, they
would tell us. Taking the name of the person most likely to make the
calls, we decided to interview one of his friends who was often in his
presence. We felt the boy we had chosen would be honest, if he had
any knowledge of any all the calls.

At approximately 1518 hrs. the student was brought into the office
and I interviewed him on record in the presence of Mr. Smith. I asked
the young man if he knew anything about any obscene phone calls
being made by any students on the date in question from the school's
payphone. He stated he overheard the conversation and he named two
brothers, our top two suspects. He stated he had just finished taking
a shower and had ask the younger of the two brothers involved to let
him borrow a hairbrush. He said he personally had no involvement in
any of the calls. He said he overheard the older of the two using pro-
fanity and then hanging up the phone, after which both the brothers
were laughing and joking around about it. The older brother dialed
the number and the younger brother put the dime in the phone so the
call could be made. He heard the older of the two brothers state he
was glad they had money to put into the phone to complete the call

this time. I thanked the young man for being honest with me and I told him he could go back to class.

The next student we brought in was the younger of the two brothers, who had been named by the witness. The principal was present during this interview, as well.

Before questioning this young man, I read him his Miranda warning. Upon completing the warning, the young man asked me how much trouble he was in. I informed him I could not question him without first having him sign his waiver. I did inform him we would be talking about some harassing and obscene phone calls which had been made recently from the payphone located outside the doorway to the gymnasium. He immediately told me he knew what I was talking about. I told him I needed his signature prior to my continuing the interview. I made it very plain what his rights were. The young man signed the waiver and I asked him to tell me what he knew about the harassing, and obscene, phone calls. He told me he and his older brother had been calling a phone number for the last week or so. He told me he did not know who the number belonged to. When asked if he had left any obscene messages, he told me he had. He said on most occasions they did not have the money to put into the phone to complete the call, so they would repeatedly just click the receiver. When asked if he did this by himself, he stated his older brother was also involved in the calls. I asked him if this was the only phone number they had been calling and he stated it was. He stated he was the one talking and left the obscene message on the telephone recorder. He said on all the other occasions there was no message because they did not have money to put into the phone.

I thanked the young man for being honest with me and told him he would most probably be hearing from Eric Weatherby, of juvenile intake office in Kenai. I told him the case was being investigated by both myself and the Homer Police Department but it was a Homer police case. I also told him the Homer police could possibly have more questions for him. I told him he should let his parents know what had taken place or if he wanted me to, I could let them know. He said he would tell them about it. I thanked him again and told him he could go back to class.

The principle, knowing his brother was in the same classroom, told him to send his older brother to the principal's office, when he got back to the classroom. The young man agreed to do so and left the office.

When the older brother reached the principal's office, I asked him to take a seat. Mr. Smith was also present during this interview.

I explained to the young man we would be talking about harassment and obscene phone calls which were being made from the payphone just outside the door to the gymnasium. I read him his Miranda warning and, unlike his brother, he readily signed his waiver of rights form without asking any questions. When asked, he outlined for me what he knew about the calls. He stated he and his brother had been making the calls for over a week now. When given the day in question, when the obscene message was made, he stated he dialed the number and his brother put the dime in to complete the connection. He said his brother was the one who did most of the talking when the obscene message was left on the phone recorder. He further stated they had been calling numerous times to the same number for over a week. On these occasions, when someone would answer, or the recorder would come on, he would repeatedly click the receiver. He said he found the number in the phone book and did not know who it belonged to but it was the only number they had been calling. I told him harassment was a crime and this type activity could result in him being confined in the juvenile detention facility where he would have no access to a telephone.

Before releasing him and letting him go back to his classroom, I informed him the Homer Police Department was the lead in this investigation and they, as well as juvenile intake, could be contacting him. I also told him he could tell his parents what was going on or I could contact them. It was mandatory they be informed so they would not be surprised if they received a phone call from either the Homer police are juvenile intake. The young man said he would convey the information to his parents. I thanked him for being honest and told him he could go back to his classroom.

Having received a confession from both suspects, I ended the investigation with regards to the Seldovia Police Department's part. I completed the necessary paperwork, with the information gained in the investigation, and faxed it to the Homer Police Department. It is unknown what the juvenile intake system did, regarding the crimes. In most cases, when dealing with juvenile intake, police departments do not usually find out what the disposition, or outcome, is. (Agency Assist, Closed by Investigation)

NOTE: *When living in a small community, such as Seldovia, an officer becomes very well acquainted with most everyone in the area. Over time the officer gains knowledge of its citizens likes, their dislikes, and their activities. This makes the officer much more aware of those in the community who have a propensity to commit criminal acts. When you consider the people those individuals associate with, you can then develop a list of suspects, as well as people you can call on when you need information. This can be critical at times and can mean the difference between solving, and not solving a case. Many times, because of the type of crime, or the severity of the crime, we can associate an activity with the younger, or teenage crowd. Other times the evidence at the crime scene will point us toward older, or more experienced participants. This knowledge becomes very beneficial when investigating most of the crimes we find ourselves dealing with. As in the previous case, it was evident to me, the harassment was most probably done by teenagers, or by younger people. Due to my being acquainted with the younger people in our community, I already had a list of suspects in mind, who would commit harassment, or make obscene phone calls, even before I arrived at the school. In the larger cities, due to the large volume of people they are dealing with, the officers investigating the crimes, do not often have these types of advantages as we do in our smaller communities. I have found throughout my career, becoming acquainted with everyone in the community, is an invaluable resource. Most of this is just a common sense approach but the relationships you build with the residents of your community play a very vital role in your ability to police your area.*

Sexual Assault of a Minor & Minors Consuming Alcohol

It was forty degrees and raining pretty heavily in Seldovia on the 21st day of April, 1991, when I was patrolling around town in the afternoon. At approximately 1:22 PM, I passed the harbor and I observed a pickup, which belong to a local teenage girl, who we will refer to as Maggie. The vehicle had its door wide open and no one around. This seemed odd so I pulled over beside the pickup to check it out. When I was exiting my patrol vehicle, I observed a three-wheeler pull up in front of the harbor master's office and an 18-year-old man, who we will refer to as Ralph, get off the machine. He walked directly into the lady's restroom. I personally knew Ralph, and after I closed the door to the vehicle, I walked over to the restroom and banged on the door with my flashlight. Ralph exited the bathroom and was immediately followed by three teenage girls. All three girls were highly intoxicated and could barely stand. Along with Maggie were two other girls, who we will refer to as Janice and Elaine. I asked Ralph what he was doing there and he stated he had been told about the girl's condition and he came to help them. I told Ralph to take off, that I would handle it from here.

I asked Maggie what was going on and she told me there was a bottle of alcohol inside the women's bathroom. She said she had gotten the bottle off of the front seat of her mother's pickup truck. I entered the bathroom and found a bottle of Jack Daniels whiskey, which had been approximately half consumed. I took the bottle as evidence.

Knowing all three girls, I did not think it necessary that I put them in handcuffs when I arrested them for minors consuming alcohol. I did, however, activate my pocket voice recorder to record any forthcoming statements. All three girls were placed in the back seat of my patrol car. I then went over to get the keys out of the Maggie's pickup truck and I found a bottle of Triple Sec whiskey lying on the seat. I took that alcohol as evidence as well. I then transported the young ladies to the Seldovia Police Department. All three girls were too intoxicated to be interviewed so I called their parents, asking them to come to the police department so I could release their daughters into their custody.

When both Janice and Elaine's parents arrived at the police department, I told each of them I would be contacting them the next day so I could conduct interviews with their daughters. I told the girl's parents they were too intoxicated to be interviewed at this time. The girls were then released into the custody of their parents.

A few minutes later Maggie's mother arrived, and she had Maggie's step-grandfather with her. As soon as Maggie saw her mother, she became very agitated. Her mother started to chastise her for drinking but Maggie yelled at her that she was screwed up because of her mother. She told her mother, because she had allowed her boyfriends to molest her in the past, her life was all screwed up. At that point Maggie began to cry. I was very interested to hear more of what Maggie was talking about but, due to her intoxicated state, I didn't know how credible her statements would be in a court of law. I made a decision not to pursue the matter at this time, but planned to take it up when I interviewed her the next day.

Maggie's step-grandfather told me Maggie lived with him now and he would see she got home safely. He said he would bring her back in tomorrow to be interviewed. I told him, the reason for my waiting to interview Maggie the next day was due to her state of intoxication. Maggie was released into the custody of her step-grandfather and they, along with Maggie's mother, left the police department.

At approximately 1422 hours, on 4/21/91, Maggie's step-grandfather brought her to the Seldovia police department to be interviewed. Maggie's mother was not with them this time. After being read her

Miranda warning, and after signing her waiver of rights, I questioned Maggie about the previous evening's activities. Maggie's step-grandfather was present during the interview.

Maggie stated the Jack Daniels whiskey was taken by her from the front seat of her mother's vehicle. She denied any knowledge of the Triple Sec whiskey, which was found in the front seat of her vehicle. I asked her if Ralph had supplied the alcohol and she said he had not. She stated all three of them were drinking from the Jack Daniels bottle. Having all the information I needed regarding the alcohol consumption, I changed my questioning, and brought up the statements she had made about her mother allowing her boyfriends to have sex with her. Maggie was presently 16 years old, but I wanted to find out how old she was when the alleged sexual assaults started. I told her she needed to address this so we could help her get through it. Maggie was very adamant, stating she did not wish to pursue the matter. I asked her if anything had actually happened or had she made it up just to get back at her mother for something. I ask her if she was angry with her mother and said these things because she was intoxicated. She assured me her mother's boyfriends had molested her on numerous occasions, but said she couldn't prove it and she did not want to pursue it. Maggie became irritated with my line of questioning so much so, I stopped pursuing it.

I informed Maggie she would be charged with minor consuming alcohol and the case would be turned over to Juvenile Intake. Eric Weatherby would, more than likely, be coming to Seldovia and she and a legal guardian would have to meet with him. I informed her, because she had not been in any trouble previously, it would be in her favor when the juvenile intake officer decided what he would do regarding her case. At that point I thanked her for being honest with me and told her if she ever felt she needed to talk to someone in confidence, I was there for her. She thanked me and she and her step-grandfather left the police department.

At approximately 1450 hours, 4/21/91, Elaine came to the police department, accompanied by her mother. As I did with Maggie, I read Elaine her Miranda Rights warning. Her mother inquired why I would read the Miranda rights to a minor and I told her I wanted to afford her all the same rights I would any adult or juvenile in any criminal matter and I wanted her to completely understand her rights. Her mother seemed satisfied with that answer and Elaine signed the waiver.

During the interview Elaine admitted to drinking both the Triple Sec and the Jack Daniels whiskey. She did, however, state she did not know where the alcohol had come from. She stated they had started drinking around noon while they were driving around in Maggie's vehicle.

I told Elaine and her mother the case would be forwarded to the Juvenile Intake Department and they would, most probably be getting contacted by Eric Weatherby, the juvenile intake officer. I told them I did not know how it would be handled but, because this is the first offense, I felt juvenile intake would take more of an educational approach than a disciplinary approach. Elaine's mother thanked me and they left the police department.

On 4/21/91, at approximately 1456 hours, Janice arrived at the police department in the presence of Elaine's mother. Janice's mother was not able to accompany her daughter due to employment responsibilities and she ask if Elaine's mother would take her place.

As in the previous interviews, I read Janice the Miranda Rights warning and she signed the waiver of rights. When I asked her to outline for me what had taken place and where the alcohol had come from, Janice told me she and the other two girls had been drinking Triple Sec, mixed with sweet and sour mix, and Jack Daniels whiskey. She stated Maggie had taken the Jack Daniels whiskey off the front seat of her mother's vehicle, and a person we will call Ann, had purchased the Triple Sec and the sweet and sour mix for them. She also stated Maggie had given Ann the money for the alcohol and Ann had traveled to the gravel pit at 1 mile to deliver the alcohol.

I informed Janice she, too, would have to meet with the Juvenile Intake Officer, Eric Weatherby. I informed her the case would be forwarded to juvenile intake for their perusal. As with the other two girls, I informed her, because this was a first offense, the juvenile intake officer would most probably make this educational rather than disciplinary. She was told, in the future, any violations would result in harsher penalties. Janice and Elaine's mother were told they could go.

At approximately 1919 hours, 4/21/91, Ann was interviewed on record at the Seldovia police department. I read her the Miranda warning and she signed her waiver of rights. I ask if she knew anything about the alcohol that had been purchased for three teenage girls and she readily admitted she had purchased a bottle of whiskey for them after they gave her the money to do so. She said the liquor was bought with a $20, bill at the Knight Spot bar. Ann stated she would not have purchased the liquor for the girls had she known they were going to drive around and drink it.

I informed Ann she would be charged with furnishing liquor to minors and she would have to go before the court to answer to those charges. I further told her I would be contacting her with a time and date of her appearance. I informed her, because she was truthful with me, I would not be arresting her on the misdemeanor charges. I was well acquainted with her and her family and knew she would not be leaving the area. I took her personal information and, even though she was not arrested, I did roll her fingerprints due to criminal charges being brought against her. When that was completed, she left the police department.

The next morning, 4/22/91, I contacted Bill Marshall, of the Division of Family and Youth Services in Homer. I relayed the information I had received regarding Maggie being sexually assaulted by her mother's boyfriends, and possibly having been exploited by her mother. I told him Maggie was very emphatic in that she did not want to pursue the matter. I also told him I did not feel qualified to investigate this case, due to the victim being hesitant to cooperate in the investigation. I felt she might be more apt to talk to someone whom she was not acquainted with, regarding the abuse. I told Bill I did not have enough experience in these type cases to take it on and I did not want to do anything which would hurt any prosecution which might come from the investigation. Bill thanked me and said he would be opening a case file and would be traveling to Seldovia in the near future. He said he would be contacting me when he would be coming over and he requested I provide transportation. I agreed and told him I would be awaiting his phone call.

I readied the case and forwarded it to Juvenile Intake in Kenai. Eric Weatherby, juvenile intake officer, did decide to handle the minor consuming cases informally, and not file any charges with the court system. Each of the minors were sent a letter, ordering them to report to SKIAP, the local alcohol program. He ordered they check in by a given date and undertake alcohol abuse counseling. He further stated SKIAP would determine how many counseling sessions they must attend, and if they did not attend the suggested number of sessions, the police department would be notified and they, in turn, would contact DFYS with the information. The letter continued that at that time, Mr. Weatherby would be filing charges with the court system and they would be required to answer to the charges of minor consuming alcohol.

I was never contacted by SKIAP in their regard so, I assume, they all finished the counseling sessions they were ordered to undertake.

Ann was given her formal complaint, as well as the time of her court appearance for arraignment on charges of furnishing liquor to minors. The arraignment was held telephonically from the police department. She pled guilty to the charge and, because she had no previous criminal convictions, was fined $250 with $150 suspended. She was placed on probation for one year and ordered to report to SKIAP to be screened for alcohol abuse and to abide by their recommendations.

This was the first time I had been involved in any criminal activity involving any of the parties involved. Because they were first-time offenders, the sentencing was light, compared to what it would have been for repeat offenders.

Bill Marshall of DFYS did come to Seldovia on 4/24/91, and did meet with Maggie, her step-grandfather and Maggie's mother. I provided transportation for Mr. Marshall and the interviews were conducted at the Seldovia police department. I did not set in on the interviews, in hopes Maggie would be more open with Mr. Marshall, without someone she was acquainted with being present. I was later informed by Mr. Marshall that he would not be pursuing any charges in the case.

He said, without the victim being willing to testify, there was no way the case could ever be brought before the court. He said it would only create more hardship for Maggie and would have the opposite result we would be seeking. Following the interviews, I provided transportation for Mr. Marshall back to the airport where he boarded an airplane and returned to Homer. (Case closed by arrest)

NOTE: *Anytime allegations are made by anyone, it is imperative that the victim stand ready to testify to the facts of the case before a court of law. If you have someone who reports a crime, which they have witnessed, or have been victimized by, but they refuse to testify, the district attorney's office will not pursue the matter. Just because someone reports a crime does not mean the crime actually occurred. Without witness testimony, or physical evidence to prove the matter, you do not have a case. As in this case, because Maggie would not testify, you cannot prove the allegations to be factual.*

The District Attorney's Office is hesitant to file cases generated by the Seldovia Police Department anyway, and to think they would prosecute a case, without the victim testifying, is certainly not going to happen.

AGENCY ASSIST - PRISONER TRANSPORT

On 4/22/91, I received a call from Trooper John Adams, of the Alaska State Troopers, from their Ninilchik post. The trooper asked me if I would be able to get free to assist him in transporting a prisoner from the Orlando, Florida area back to Anchorage. He said the Troopers were shorthanded and, since I was a commissioned trooper, and had worked with them for so many years, his superiors had suggested they ask me if I would like to go along. He said the prisoner had to be transported from the Kissimmee Correctional Facility in Kissimmee, Florida to Anchorage, to stand trial on charges of robbery in the 2nd degree. I asked him how long we would be gone on the trip and he said he was taking a week, which he thought would be adequate time. I told Trooper Adams I would have to check with the city manager but, I told him, I would see if I could get clearance to go, and that I would very much like to make the trip with him. I told him I would let him know as soon as I found out. He said, if I could work it out, we would be leaving on the evening of the 24th, out of Anchorage, just two days from today. He told me he would pick me up in Homer and we would drive to Anchorage, where we would catch our flight to Florida.

I left the police department and drove to the city offices, where I contacted the city manager. I told the manager what the Alaska State Troopers had asked of me and he told me if I did not have anything pending which would prohibit it, I was cleared to go. I immediately returned to the police department and called Trooper Adams to let him know I had been cleared to go with him on the trip. He said I should probably take the first flight, from Seldovia to Homer, on the morning of the 24th so we could get on the road as early as possible. I told him I would make arrangements and keep him updated as to my schedule. I asked Trooper Adams if I should carry my weapon with me on the trip. He said he had been given a special clearance to be armed but I had not been cleared and it would probably take too long to get the clearance, so I would have to travel unarmed.

For the rest of the day, and on the day following, I caught up the loose ends I had pending. I made arrangements to take the first flight, with Homer Airlines, to Homer on the morning of the 24th. I then packed my suitcase for the trip. My wife jokingly told me she did not know about my going to Florida with John Adams. She said when the two of us got together, there was no telling what would happen.

John Adams was a very likable and funny guy. He was a total pleasure to be around and was always coming up with something off-the-wall. Anyone in John's presence certainly was never bored but, at the same time, you had to be on your toes. He had a mischievous streak and you never knew what he would come up with next. Needless to say, I was looking forward to this trip.

John picked me up at the Homer Airlines office at 9:00 AM on the morning of the 24th, in his trooper vehicle. He told me arrangements had already been made for our transportation, from Anchorage to Orlando, Florida, and the tickets were waiting for us at the Alaska Airlines counter. He said we would be leaving Anchorage this evening and we would be flying to Seattle, Washington, where we would change aircraft. We would then be routed through Atlanta, Georgia, where we would, again, change airplanes, to complete our trip to Orlando. From there we would rent a car to drive to Kissimmee.

On our trip to Anchorage John and I reminisced about old cases and all the friends we had in common, who were mostly cops. I have little doubt, many police officer's ears were burning on that day. John had been a trooper for many years and his stories, even though somewhat embellished had some element of truth to them. The four-hour trip to Anchorage seemed to pass quickly.

We made the flight out of Anchorage to Seattle without any complications and boarded our flight to Atlanta. The trip to Atlanta took over five hours and John and I continued to visit throughout most of the flight. When we reached Atlanta, it was after midnight and we were both pretty tired. We walked to our gate and, when they called for our flight, we boarded and took our seats. Both John and I tried to get some sleep, but I do not sleep well on airplanes and I hardly got any rest at all. John, on the other hand, seemed to sleep like a baby for most of the flight. When I mentioned I could not sleep very well on an airplane, John said most people with shady pasts, and the guilty conscience, have a hard time sleeping. Of course, he chuckled at his own statement, which he thought was very humorous.

By the time we reached the Orlando airport, I just wanted to find a place to lay down, however, that was not happening. We rented the vehicle, for the trip to Kissimmee. John drove and it was midmorning by the time we reached Kissimmee. We stopped at a motel and took a room. John told me we would check in with the correctional facility the next morning and let them know we were in town. We both caught a shower and got a few hours' sleep. John had informed me our flight back, with the prisoner, was scheduled for mid-day on March 28th, so we had some time to kill. After a few hours' sleep, we got up and drove around and located a restaurant, where we stopped and ate dinner. Still being somewhat drug out from the flight, we went back to the room, following dinner, watched a little TV, then went to bed.

The next morning John called the correctional facility and told them we were in town and asked them if anything had changed, reference our flight back. He was told nothing had changed and they told him they would see us on the morning of the 28th. Being only the 26th day of April, we had a couple days to kill, so we drove around sightseeing until mid-afternoon.

There is a large lake in the Kissimmee area and we had noticed there were a number of bass boats in the area, being pulled by high dollar pickup trucks. Around mid-afternoon we stopped at a tackle/bait shop and asked the man behind the counter if there were any bass charter outfits in the area. He said there were a number of charters, but he recommended one he said most always produced for his clients. John got the telephone number from the attendant and called the guy from a pay phone located in front of the tackle/bait shop. John made contact with the guy and arrangements were made for us to go on a bass fishing charter and we were to leave the dock area at 8:30 AM, the next morning. John ask the man what we should bring along, and he was told we would be out for around four hours, so if we wanted, we could bring drinks and a sandwich or snack. John was told where we would meet the boat the next morning. We left the tackle/bait shop and drove to the lake, so we would be sure we knew where to go the following morning. That evening at dinner John said he would bet me a steak dinner he would catch the biggest fish. Of course, being somewhat competitive, I was not about to turn that down. I could not let a state trooper beat me, so the bet was on. I told John my steak would taste so much better just knowing he was paying for it. John said he had not lost a bet in 10 years, and no two-bit city cop was going to break his record. I told him, again, how good the steak, he was going to buy me, would taste and I told him, while I was eating steak, he'd be eating crow.

The next morning, bright and early, we got up and went to a restaurant and had breakfast. We arrived at the boat dock at approximately 8:15 AM. The charter operator had not yet arrived. We were both chomping at the bit to get underway. Just prior to our departure time, a very fancy painted, newer pickup truck, pulling a fiberglass speedboat, which perfectly matched the paint scheme of the pickup, arrived and was launched from the launch ramp. The boat operator boarded the speedboat and drove over to the dock where John and I were waiting. He introduced himself as Jack and ask if we were his clients. We acknowledge we were and, after becoming acquainted, we boarded the boat and got underway.

The wind was blowing approximately 15 to 20 miles an hour and, even in Florida, I found it to be a little chilly. Neither John nor I brought anything more than a light jacket to wear, and we were wishing we had packed something a little heavier. The boat must have reached speeds of 35 to 40 mile per hour and, with the wind blowing, we had to hold onto our hats to keep from losing them.

For over an hour we fished, without getting any bites at all. We changed locations a number of times and Jack kept changing our bait, but nothing seemed to do any good. Jack told us the wind had a real effect on bass, and they sometimes were not feeding when it was blustery. John was the first to catch a small bass, but it was only around five inches in length. Of course, I gave him a hard time about catching baby fish with milk still on their lips. He had some comment to the effect, that his fish was a lot bigger than any of mine, and he again chuckled. After approximately another hour, I finally got a hit, and caught a fish, but it was only an inch or so larger than John's. Of course, John commented about mine still being in diapers. Even though it was windy, and we were not getting many strikes, we were enjoying ourselves. After coming from 40 to 45-degree weather in Alaska, we were enjoying the 65 to 70-degree weather in Florida, even with the wind. Had the wind not been blowing, it would have been much warmer, if not too hot. The sun was shining and we could feel the heat through our clothing.

Jack was also fishing, but he was not having any luck at all. He had not landed a fish all morning. Approximately 45 minutes to an hour before we headed back in, John landed another bass. Of course, he was laughing and taunting me while he pulled the fish in. This one was nearly 10 inches long, but the way John was carrying on, one would have thought it was a world record. I should have cut his stinking line. Long story short, I bought John a steak dinner with all the trimmings that evening. He was gloating so much during the meal I was surprised he didn't choke. He certainly got a lot of mileage out of that little bitty tiny fish he landed. You would not believe how much that fish had grown by the time we got back to Alaska and he related the story to some of his friends. I am not one to say John would actually be untruthful about anything, but I certainly have witnessed him embellish many of his stories. This was just one more story he could embellish. I chuckle just thinking about all the fun we had on that trip. Of course, when John told the story, with all of his embellishments, you probably would not recognize it as even being the same trip.

John and I got up bright and early the next morning and had breakfast, before going to the Kissimmee Correctional Facility. When we were underway to the jail facility, John, in one of his rare serious moments, shared with me he was a little concerned regarding problems occurring during the transport of the prisoner. He said, if the inmate had friends who tried to break him out, they would attempt it, most likely, at the Orlando Airport. I told John I did not see that as a problem. I suggested, when we get to the airport, he should handcuff the prisoner to my right arm and I would guarantee the prisoner would not run off or be taken very easily by his friends. John, being John, laughed and said, "Why didn't I think of that. Even if they did shoot you, the prisoner still could not go anywhere." He said, "He would be anchored, and if they did start shooting, I could just hide behind you." I looked at John and just shook my head. We both laughed, conjuring up that scenario in our minds. John never missed an opportunity to be humorous, and he was so quick witted, you never knew what he would come up with.

Upon arrival at the correctional facility, we were taken into a waiting room, and after approximately 10 minutes, the inmate was delivered to where we were waiting. John exchanged the facilities handcuffs with his own and was then given the necessary paperwork for the transfer. The prisoner was approximately 5'7" to 5'8" tall and was of a slight build, weighing probably not more than 170 pounds. John was probably about the same height and weight as the inmate but I, being 6' 3" tall, and weighing well in excess of 250 pounds, was much more of an intimidating figure than was Trooper Adams. As serious as he could, John told the inmate it was going to be a long trip back to Anchorage, and hopefully, there would be no problems between Kissimmee and Anchorage. Pointing at me, he asked the inmate, "Do you see that big fellow there? Well," John said, "I brought him along to take care of any problems that might arise and it is probably in your best interest that you do not piss him off." The inmate assured John there would be no problems. John told him, that was good, because I was a lot meaner than I looked. John looked at me, with a big smile on his face and a mischievous look in his eye and told the inmate, "In reality, I'm the muscle and he's really the brains of this outfit." I'm sure he had the guy totally confused at this point.

After all the paperwork was in place, and the prisoner was made ready for travel, we escorted him to the waiting rental car, where he and I took up the back seat. John drove from Kissimmee to the airport in Orlando. We were on the road approximately 45 minutes when the inmate asked where we were going. John told him we were going to the Orlando airport. The inmate said, "Well you passed the airport exit 10 to 15 minutes ago." Of course, both John and I were totally new to the area, but we could not believe we had passed the airport, with all the signs indicating the airport exits. John took the next exit, turned around and headed back in the direction of Orlando. The signs, directing us to the airport, were very large and very easily followed. I don't know how we missed seeing the exit sign when we were headed north. Thank goodness we had left early enough to allow a buffer.

We reached the Orlando airport and turned in the rental car and then made our way to the airlines ticket counter. Without any more problems, we were able to reach the gate and board the aircraft. Because we were accompanying a prisoner, we were placed in the rear row of seats in the aircraft. We put the inmate in the center seat, with John taking the seat by the window and me setting in the seat on the isle. During the flight the inmate and John played cribbage. They must have played 30 or 40 games between Orlando and Anchorage.

The inmate seemed to be a very likable fellow and never gave us any problems at all. It was a long trip back to Anchorage, with two airplane changes, but we made all the connections without incident. I think the trip felt much shorter for John and the inmate than it did for me, by them having played games all the way.

After we reached Anchorage International Airport, John and I escorted the prisoner to where the trooper vehicle had been stored. We then transported him to the jail facility and John took him inside while I waited in the vehicle.

After the prisoner had been released into the custody of the jail, John and I headed for Homer. It was only shortly afternoon by this time and we had enough time to reach Homer, and if the weather cooperated, I could get a flight to Seldovia before dark. Luckily, the weather did cooperate and I was able to get home. Trooper Adams thanked me for accompanying him on the trip and told me he had very much enjoyed the trip and maybe someday we could do it again. He did reiterate, however, that he would never forget how good that steak dinner tasted.

Many times, I have been involved with the Alaska State Troopers, wherein we have worked together on a number of different cases, however, this was the first time I had ever taken an extended trip with another cop. I can say, unequivocally, one would have to go a long way to ever top this trip I took with a brother in arms. The only thing that would have made the trip any better, would have been if it had lasted longer, and maybe, if I had caught a larger fish than John.

I am sure those of you who personally know John Adams, are more than aware of his mischievous ways, his spontaneous humor and his love of life. I am so glad I did not pass up this trip with Trooper Adams and, in the future, if I were ever to be invited again, I would not hesitate to take another such trip with this man. I have heard many stories about his life and his escapades, and I am sure, if a biography were ever written about John Adams, it would be a hilarious best seller. I got to know John much better on this trip, and I am proud to call him friend.

CRIMINAL MISCHIEF

On 5/22/91, I was contacted by Frank Monsey, the fire chief, at approximately 1405 hours reporting he was at the Seldovia boat harbor and requested I respond to that location. He said a number of the fire extinguishers on the boat harbor had been tampered with, which created a real hazard for boat owners and for the City of Seldovia were a fire to occur. I immediately left the police department and drove to the boat harbor where I met with Mr. Monsey.

When I met with him, I was told a fire extinguisher on "A" float had been emptied and seven more fire extinguishers on "A," "B," "C" and "D" floats had been tampered with, having their pins removed. He said an electrician, who had been hired by the city and was working in the boat harbor, had seen a teenage boy showing another boy how to activate the fire extinguisher which was emptied on "A" float.

At approximately 1415 hours I contacted the electrician in the Seldovia boat harbor, and he told me he had observed a tour boat pull in and tie up to the float. He said a number of youngsters had gotten off the boat and two of the boys had gone to a fire extinguisher on "A" float. The electrician stated he heard one of the young boys tell the other he would show him how the fire extinguisher worked. He said the boy then pulled the pin on the extinguisher and activated it, releasing the powder. He described the boy that activated the fire extinguisher as wearing a dark coat, trimmed in a fluorescent color. He said the other young man was wearing a white stocking cap with designs on it.

I contacted the chaperone, who had brought his Project Adventure class to Seldovia, and told him what had taken place. The chaperone was very helpful throughout the investigation and was present when I interviewed all the suspects. When the two student's clothing was described to him, he knew immediately who the students were.

At approximately 1431 hours, in the presence all the chaperone, a young man who we will call Ronald, was questioned on "E" float, in the Seldovia boat harbor. Upon being asked what had taken place reference the fire extinguisher, he said he and another boy, who we will call Kenneth, exited the boat and went to "A" float, where Kenneth activated the fire extinguisher. Ronald said he did not know why Kenneth had activated the fire extinguisher, but he did not touch it and was only watching.

At approximately 1452 hours, I interviewed Kenneth, in the police vehicle with the chaperone being present. Kenneth said he had only pushed on the handle of the fire extinguisher and the pin was already missing. He named two other students, who we will call Bob and Zack, stating they had pulled a number of pins out of fire extinguishers on a number of the floats in the harbor. He said the students had been collecting the fire extinguisher pins for quite a while. He named other towns where the students had pulled extinguisher pins and said they would probably have their pin collections at their homes. He denied having any fire extinguisher pins on him or having pulled any of the pins.

At approximately 1521 hours, Zach was interviewed in the police vehicle at the Seldovia harbor, with the chaperone being present during the questioning. Zack admitted to pulling three pins out of fire extinguishers located on floats "A," "B" and "C" floats, but stated he replaced all three pins which he had removed. He said Bob was with him and he had also pulled three pins out of the extinguishers on those floats. He said, even though he put his back, he thought Bob had kept his pins. Zach said, a boy we'll call James, was also involved in pulling the pins from "D" float, but he did not know how many.

At approximately 1700 hours, Bob was interviewed at the Seldovia police department, in the presence of the chaperone. When told the officer had information he had taken three pins out of the fire extinguishers on the different floats, Bob readily admitted it. When asked if he still had the three pins, he told the officer they were in his backpack at the school. Bob told the officer he and Zack were together when the fire extinguisher pins were removed. Bob later returned the fire extinguisher pins he had stated were in his backpack at the school.

At approximately 1712 hours, in the presence of the class chaperone, I interviewed James at the Seldovia police department. James admitted to pulling two fire extinguisher pins from extinguishers located on "D" float, but stated that he had thrown them away after he heard the police were looking into the pins being taken.

Following the interview with James, I requested the chaperone have all the boys come to the Seldovia Police Department, where I could tell them what was going to take place. Each time I interviewed one of the boys, I took his personal information for the case, so I had all the information I needed to complete the case.

At approximately 2040 hours, after all the boys were gathered at the police department, with their chaperone, I told them this was a very serious game they were playing. Had there been a fire in the harbor, after the extinguishers had been deactivated, millions of dollars of damage could have occurred, not to mention the possible loss of lives. I explained to them the first 15 to 20 minutes of a fire, in a boat harbor, are fought with these fire extinguishers, which are kept on the boat floats for that specific purpose. I further told them, if there was a fire which caused considerable damage, and if the authorities could find out who had disabled the fire extinguishers, they, and their families, could be held liable for the cost of replacement. This includes both the boat float and any boats damaged or lost. To further get my point across, I told them if a life were lost, they could be held criminally liable. In other words, I told him, they could be arrested and charged with homicide. Before they were released, they were informed I would be sending this case to Juvenile Intake in Kenai and they would most likely be hearing from Eric Weatherby, the juvenile intake officer. They would then have to answer for their part in this criminal activity. I told them the crime, at this point, is labeled Criminal Mischief, and thank goodness nothing more had occurred, while the fire extinguishers were inoperative.

The chaperone told the boys to go back to the school and to stay there until he arrived. After they were gone, he thanked me for getting to the bottom of this activity and ask if I would be contacting the other cities where this had occurred. I assured him I would be in touch with the police departments in those other areas. He said he hoped the boys would see the seriousness of their actions and start thinking before doing these sorts of things. I thanked him for all his help in the investigations, and we shook hands, and he left the police department.

I put the case together and forwarded it to the juvenile intake division, but like in most juvenile cases, I never did find the complete disposition of the case. I do know the boys were required to pay restitution for the loss of the pins, the re-charging of the empty fire extinguishers, which had been emptied, plus the freight to and from Homer. They also had to pay for the fire chiefs time for all the hours he spent on the case. The loss totaled $308.48. The fire chief later told me he had received two checks for restitution but was still waiting for three more from the other students involved. (Case Closed by Investigation and Referral to Juvenile Intake)

NOTE: *During the summer of 1991, the police department stayed busy with calls for assistance, animal control complaints, traffic enforcement and a myriad of other responses, plus the daily functions of the department. The fourth of July was very busy in 1991 and we found ourselves putting in a very long day. I lead the parade in the morning and responded to numerous calls throughout the day and into the night. Many of the calls were noise complaints or alcohol related complaints. One report was of a baby crying aboard a locked boat. I responded to the harbor and unlocked the door on the boat and the baby was all alone, lying on the bed crying. The mother of the child showed up at the boat approximately 10 minutes later, and I questioned why she would leave the baby aboard a boat unattended. She stated she had to go to the restroom and the baby was sleeping when she left. She said she had been gone no longer than 15 minutes but I corrected her, telling her we had been aboard longer than 15 minutes. I took her personal information and told her I did not want to see the child unattended again, while she was in Seldovia. The next* morning, during regular business hours, I contacted the division of family and your services and sent them a copy of the incident report. The lady and her husband lived in Homer and DFYS was located in the city as well. I was never told what action, was taken by DFYS, but hopefully they did look into the matter.

Other than that incident, nothing of any major significance occurred that is noteworthy. However, the never-ending paperwork did not seem to slow down, so the officers never found themselves lacking for something to do.

DC, Minor Consuming Alcohol, Weapons Misconduct 3ʳᵈ Degree

I t was 2335 hours, on Sunday, 10/13/91, when a concerned mother called on the police telephone reporting a young man was trying to start a fight with her son, and his two friends out in front of her house located on Seldovia Street. She said the young man was swinging's sticks over his head, which resembled num-chucks, and he was yelling profanities at the three boys. She told me she had yelled at the young man to leave and he had gone, only to return a short time later and resume his challenges towards all the three boys, challenging them to fight with him.

I called Officer John Gruber on the radio and told him about the call and then swung by his house and picked him up, and we both responded to the call. Upon arrival at the scene I observed a young man, who we will call Larry, dressed in camouflage coat and pants, standing near the entry way of the complainant's home. Just inside the foyer of the complainant's home, I observed the complainant's son and his two friends. I exited my vehicle and instructed Larry to put both hands on top of his head and interlock his fingers. He turned toward me and reluctantly did as directed. As I walked up to him, I told him to turn around away from me, but he didn't comply. I took him by the elbow and turned him around and told him to stay in that position, while I patted him down. When I patted him down, I found a survival knife in his sheath on his belt, and a stainless steel, Kitchen Delight, butcher knife, with a 9-inch blade, located on the inside pocket of his coat. One of the young men inside the foyer volunteered that Larry had thrown the num-chucks under a car, which was parked in front of the residence, when he observed us coming. Officer Gruber looked under the vehicle and found the num-chucks. The officer retrieved the num-chucks, to be taken as evidence. I smelled a strong odor of alcohol on Larry. I also observed his eyes were bloodshot and his face appeared flushed. When I attempted to question him, he was cocky and argumentative, even belligerent at times and his voice was slurred. There was no question, he was under the influence of alcohol.

I asked Larry what was going on, why was he trying to cause problems with the three teenagers. He said they were picking on him and he was only defending himself. When told I smelled alcohol on his breath, he told me he had found a bottle of liquor and had drank it. I asked him what kind of liquor and he said he didn't know.

I arrested Larry, and placed him in handcuffs, and transported him to the Seldovia Police Department. The num-chucks, the butcher knife, along with the knife in the sheath were all taken as evidence. Upon entry to the police department I activated a voice recorder, to record any upcoming statements. I read Larry his Miranda rights warning and he refused to sign the waiver of rights. He said he wanted to talk to an attorney he had in Michigan before signing anything. I told him he was an adult, 18 years of age, and he would be charged as an adult, with minor consuming alcohol, and he would be placed in the cell, regardless of whether he talked to his attorney or not. At this point he was booked and placed in the jail cell. Five minutes had passed, after being placed in the cell, when Larry attempted to break out the cell window, with the chair we kept in the cell. I unlocked the door and entered the cell, taking both the chair and the table out. This left him only the bunk, or the commode, to set on. The plastic that covered the window to the cell was a high dollar, unbreakable plastic, and no damage had occurred to the plastic or the window. When I was removing the chair and table, Larry attempted to run out of the jail cell. Because he was being erratic, I grabbed him and handcuffed him to the upright post which held up the two bunks. He could not hurt himself from that position. Being handcuffed, as he was, left him with the ability to set, or lie down, on either the lower or the upper bunk. Shortly after I exited the cell, with the chair and the table, Larry attempted to kick out the light fixture, while lying on the top bunk. I reentered the cell and I then handcuffed him to the upright on the lower bunk, where he could not reach the light fixture. Larry stayed in that position for the rest of the night and there were no further problems. A jail guard was called to come in and guard the prisoner for the night.

I called the three teenagers in and I interviewed them each separately. The first teenager interviewed told me Larry had approached the three of them while they were out in front of the complainant's home, and he had a bottle of Bacardi rum and some Pepsi with him. He felt Larry was intoxicated and said he was overly aggressive and threatening all three of them. He said the complainant yelled at Larry to leave and he had gone away for a few minutes, only to return with a pair of num-chucks. The teenager said Larry was swinging them around and continued challenging the three of them to fight. At one point the teenager said Larry told him he heard he was a narc. Larry also told them he'd had a dream wherein his father had died in Vietnam and he had been given his father's powers. He also told the three of them he had been married at one time, but he had killed his wife. He said he had spotted the handle of the knife, inside Larry's coat, as well as the knife which was in the sheath on his hip. He said Larry, when arguing with them, kept snapping the sheath open and closed on the knife he was wearing on his belt. When asked, the teenager stated he did feel, had the police not arrived when they did, a fight would have surely ensued.

Upon interviewing the two other teenagers, I found all their stories to be pretty much identical. There was no doubt the three teenagers were telling the total truth. They had no time to have rehearsed their statements, given the time frame between its occurrence and the time of the interviews. All three of the teenagers reported all the facts identically.

The boys were told they could leave and the complainant was asked to come in for an interview. She was also interviewed on record. Like the other three statements, she said she heard the yelling and saw the num-chucks being swung around while Larry was threatening the three boys. She was convinced a fight would have occurred, had the police not arrived when they did. She told me she thought the boy was either intoxicated or crazy.

At approximately 1030 hours, the following morning, after the paperwork had been filed with the court, Larry was arraigned on charges of disorderly conduct, minor consuming alcohol and misconduct involving weapons in the 3rd degree. The arraignment was held telephonically from the Seldovia police department. Larry pled not guilty and the cases were set over for trial at a later date. After I outlined what had taken place, the judge set Larry's bail at $2500 cash only. He could not make bail so I called the airlines and transported him to the Homer jail facility, where he would be held pending trial. In approximately 10 days he would be given a bail review hearing, at which time his bail could be reduced or he could be released on his own recognizance.

At his bail review hearing Larry was able to make bail and he was released from the Homer jail. Larry, however, did not show up for his trial date and warrants were issued for his arrest.

I never heard if Larry was ever brought before the court, on the charges I levied against him. I also don't know if he was ever arrested on the outstanding warrants. I'm sure, given the inner workings of all the police departments across the nation, any contact Larry has with police, would result in his outstanding warrants popping up. (Case closed by arrest)

NOTE: *When an outstanding warrant is served, the arresting agency is responsible for the removal of the warrant from the computer. This ensures the subject would not again be arrested on that same offense. Any police agency can, at any time, check the computer to see if the person, named in the original warrant, has been arrested or not. I personally never did check to see if Larry's warrant was still in effect, or if he had been arrested pursuant to it. So, it's likely, with Larry's attitude, he would have had contact with other police officers after he left Seldovia. On most stops, or contacts, the officer has reason to run those he stops for any outstanding warrants. In some police department it's a policy and the officers are instructed to run anyone he/she contacts. It is more than likely Larry was arrested and did have to answer to the charges I levied against him. However, with the district attorney's, and the defense attorneys, being in agreement to lighten the load on the court, Larry could very well have had his charges reduced and/or dismissed. Regardless, the Seldovia police department did our job and kept our citizens safe and we cannot be held responsible for the District Attorney's Office, or the court system.*

DWI & Failure to Wear a Seatbelt

It was Sunday, 10/27/91, and it was approximately 40 degrees with light rain falling, when I received a call at approximately 10 minutes after midnight, from my patrol officer, who will refer to as C-3. He was calling to inform me he was in pursuit of a pickup truck which had left the Seldovia Lodge and was failing to stop for his overhead lights and siren. Having not yet gone to bed, I started gearing up to respond. When I was headed out the door, I observed C-3's patrol vehicle to be stopped by the stop sign, on the south side of the intersection of Alder and Seldovia Street. Even though it was dark, I could see a pickup truck at the northwest corner of the police department. Both vehicles were stopped and, being able to see with the streetlights, I observed the officer to be at the driver's window of the pickup. He appeared to be talking to someone inside. The police department was only one block west of my residence on Alder Street. I quickly responded to the location with my patrol vehicle and found the pickup had been driven into the corner of the police department. When I exited my vehicle, I observed C-3 standing at the open door of the pickup truck and he was ordering the occupant out the vehicle. I walked up behind the officer and I immediately recognized the driver. The man was a local resident, who had lived in Seldovia most of his life. He was telling the officer he was not going to get out of the vehicle and said he was going to go home. Having known the man for many years, I suggested C-3 let me talk to him. C-3 stepped back and I walked up to the door, and calling the man by name, asked him to step out of the vehicle. He told me the same thing he had told my officer, that he was going to go home. He then reached for the ignition and was going to start the pickup truck. I quickly reached in and removed his hand off the ignition and took the keys out of the vehicle. At that point, the subject grabbed me by my coat and I reacted, physically pulling him from the vehicle and pushing him face first into the side of the vehicle. I observed a strong odor of alcohol on him and I observed him to slur his words when he spoke. He also had difficulty in maintaining his balance. I told him to settle down, but he was belligerent and becoming combative. He would not take direction, but I was able, after a time, to calm him down where I could communicate somewhat with him. I asked him if he would submit to field sobriety test. He told me he was not taking any tests. I then ask him if he would submit to a portable breath test (PBT), and he refused that as well. I asked him to put his arms behind his back and I placed him in handcuffs. I then informed him he was under arrest for driving while intoxicated. Closer evaluation revealed he was most probably too intoxicated for me to even attempt any field sobriety tests. I instructed C-3 to transport the subject to the jail facility. It was only approximately 50 yards to the front door of the police department but I didn't want to have to carry the man. C-3 took the subject by the arm and walked him to his patrol vehicle and helped him into the passenger side front seat.

I pulled my vehicle around to the east side of the building, near the entry door, and went inside the police department. After I entered, I turned on the voice recorder, to record any upcoming statements. C-3 brought the suspect to the police department and into my office, where he set him in a chair facing my desk. C-3 then informed me he had observed the subject leave the Seldovia Lodge, where he ran the stop sign at Young Street and Anderson Way. He then observed him cross the road, drive off the roadway into the ditch on the east side of the roadway. The officer said the suspect was then able to steer the pickup back onto Anderson Way and continue on in a southerly direction. He said the suspect then drove off the West side of Anderson Way, into the ditch, but was, again, able to steer back onto the roadway and continue in a southerly direction. C-3 said the suspect swerved back and forth on the roadway and then ran the stop sign at the intersection of Anderson Way at Alder Street. The suspect then continued across Alder Street, and due to his inebriated state, ran over the stop sign on east corner of Alder Street at Seldovia Street. Immediately after running over the stop sign, the subject turned the vehicle to the left, possibly attempting to turn easterly onto Alder Street, in the direction of his home, and he drove into the corner of the building that houses the police department. C-3 stated he then observed him back up approximately two car lengths and then run into the corner of the building a second time. Due to a flower bed being attached to the building, no damage to the building was sustained. C-3 said there was considerable damage to the right front grill and fender of the subject's vehicle, as well as the fan and radiator. The officer said he didn't think the vehicle would have started, had the subject been able to continue his attempt.

After the officer related his observations to me, I read the subject is Miranda warning. He refused to sign his waiver of rights. Even though the subject was highly intoxicated, I again asked him if he would submit to a series of field sobriety tests. He again refused any field sobriety test but, surprisingly, when asked to submit to a breath test, the subject complied. After I had observed him for approximately 20 minutes, to ensure he had nothing in his mouth, I administered an Intoximeter breath test. The test resulted in a finding of .396 blood alcohol content. The subject had admitted to drinking four or five beers but, with that high of a blood alcohol, he probably had three to four times that much to drink. Most people would be comatose at that blood alcohol level. I certainly understood why he was so unsteady on his feet.

The necessary paperwork was completed and the subject's fingerprints were taken and he was put through the booking process. I administratively revoked the subject's operator's license and gave him a temporary seven-day license. As per policy, bail was set at $500 cash. The subject called a friend, who came down and fronted him the bail money. He was given a court date when he would be arraigned on the DWI charges. He was told he could appear telephonically, from the Seldovia Police Department at that time and date, or he could appear in Homer court. Prior to releasing him, a citation was issued for his failure to wear a seatbelt. The bail for not wearing a seatbelt was only $15 and he was told he could pay that directly to the fire department and get a receipt to prove payment. He was told he had 30 days to either address the court or pay the fine in that regard.

The subject did appear before the court telephonically, from the Seldovia police department and he pled guilty to DWI. The judge fined him $500 with $250 suspended, sentenced him to 45 days in jail with 42 suspended, ordered him to report to SKIAP following court today, and sign up for their alcohol program, which could include up to 30 days of residential treatment. He was also placed on probation for two years and the judge ordered his operator's license to be revoked for 90 days. Restitution in the amount of $100 was to be paid to the Department of Transportation for the damaged stop sign, and was to be paid within one month. The subject had already paid his $15 to the fire department for his seat belt violation and he produced a receipt to the police department as proof of payment. Following arraignment, the subject left the police department. (Case closed by arrest)

CHILD ABUSE AND
CHILD NEGLECT REPORT

On 11/11/91, at approximately 1300 hours, I received a telephone call from a concerned lady in Anchorage, who had been talking to her half-sister, who lived in Seldovia. She said she felt her half-sister was in need of police assistance. She had received a call from her half-sister at 8:30 AM and she was told her half-sister had been kicked her out of the house by her father, after he discovered she had not done the dishes. The caller said her half-sister was very distraught and did not know what she was going to do. When she asked her if she thought her father was serious, her half-sister told her he said for her to pack her bags and to get out. She received another call at noon today, she said, stating her mother was packing her bags and she did not know where she was going to live. The caller said she was safe, at this time, because she was in school. The caller also said she was told her half-brother, who also lives at that residence, had a bruise on his back, from where his father had gotten mad and hit him. The caller was very worried about both her half-sister and her half-brother, and requested police ensure the children's safety.

Immediately after talking to the caller, I responded to the school and talked with Mike Smith, the school principal. I outlined the allegations which had been made and told him I needed to speak with both of the children, to ascertain if the information was factual or not. I also told Mr. Smith, I wanted to interview them separately and I requested he be present during the interviews.

Before interviewing the two youngsters, I called Ron Harper of the Division of Family and Youth Services (DFYS) in Homer and made him aware of the allegations. Ron told me to let him know what was said, after conducting my interviews. He stated, if it were ascertained the two were in danger, we would certainly remove them from the home to ensure the children's safety. He also told me their father, who will refer to as Alex, needed to be informed regarding state law and about his financial responsibility concerning their care, were he to kick them out of the home. He said he would be awaiting my phone call, following the interviews.

At approximately 1:25 PM I interviewed the half-sister of the complainant in the principal's office, with the principal being present. I told the girl, I had information indicating she had been kicked out of her home by her father and she did not know where she was going to go. She said her father angers easily and he had gotten angry because she had not done the dishes. She said he told her to get out when he was angry. She also told me Alex did not mean it and she was going to go home after school was out. She told me she was not afraid to go home and she had never been beaten or abused by her father. I told her I had also heard her brother had a bruise on his back, which had been inflicted by her father. She told me her brother had eaten a lot of candy after he had been told not to and her father had gotten angry and had spanked him with a belt. When asked how Alex had applied the belt, she said she was upstairs and did not see the spanking but she did hear it. She said the mark on her brother's back was only red, but she and her mother thought it may turn into a bruise.

Before ending the interview, I told the girl the police were very concerned about her and her brother's safety. I told her I knew her father very well and I knew, at times, he becomes volatile. I also conveyed to her, even a parent cannot assault or abuse their children, and if she ever needed answers to any questions, or was in fear for her safety, or the safety of others in her household, she could call me at any time, day or night.

At approximately 1:35 PM the girl's brother was summoned to the principal's office and I interviewed him with Mike Smith present, as well as the student counselor. I told the young man I had heard he had a bruise on his back which was a result of him being punished by his father. The boy said he had received a whipping on Saturday after he and his younger sister had eaten some candy after they were told not to. He assured me he was not ever struck with the buckle on the belt, and he further assured me, he was not afraid of his father and did not fear going home after school. When asked, he stated he could not remember the last time his father had given him a whipping. I told the boy; I was very concerned for his safety because I knew how volatile his father could get. I also told him, he could feel free to call on me with any questions, or for any assistance he might need at any time, day or night. I assured him I would keep in confidence any conversation we had and no one would be told about the call. I also told him, sometimes parents need to be educated in how to control their anger, and with the counseling, they often learn how to deal with the issues and avoid becoming so angry. Before ending the interview, I told the young man, if he ever felt in fear for his safety at any time, and needed to leave his home to be safe, all he had to do was contact me. I ask the boy if I could check to see if you bruise on his back, as was reported. Upon lifting his shirt, I observed a red mark, which was consistent with being hit by a belt, but there was no bruising. He thanked me and said he would call if he needed to. The young man then returned to his classroom.

At approximately 2:41 PM, 11/11/91, I contacted Alex at the Seldovia Lodge and informed him I had talked to both of his children at the school. I told him I had been informed he had kicked his daughter out of the home, for not doing the dishes. Alex's temper immediately flared and he inquired as to who had reported he had kicked his daughter out. I told him the source of the information would remain confidential. He said he only told her that to scare her into doing the dishes. He said if the kids were going to participate in sports, they had to help around the house. He told me he loved his children and would never kick them out of the house. I made Alex aware of his financial responsibility for his children, if they were kicked out. I told him he would be responsible for them until they were 18 years of age.

I also told Alex I had gained information, his son may have received a bruise, when he was hit by his father recently, but I had checked and only found a red mark on his back. Alex said his son and his younger sister had eaten 12 pounds of candy and then the boy lied to him when confronted. He said this was discovered after he took his son to the doctor for appendicitis and his pain turned out to be the result of him eating too much candy. He said when they got home, he had spanked the boy with his belt, and he did not feel he had done anything wrong. Alex again insisted I tell him who was reporting all these things about him. He said it had just happened this morning and he had not told anyone about it. I told him my sources would remain confidential, and it was not important who called. What was important was there were persons who were concerned enough to call the police.

After my having talked with Alex, I responded to the police department where I again called DFYS and talked with Ron Harper. I told him what I had found out and we concluded there was not enough evidence to pursue the matter. Both the daughter and son denied being afraid to go home and also denied being afraid of their father. Both denied their father ever physically abused them and there was no evidence to prove otherwise. There was no bruise on the boys back, although there were red marks which were indicative of being struck with a belt. Alex readily admitted he had spanked his son with his belt but did not feel he had done anything wrong. Ron requested I send him a copy of the case, even though it was not going to be pursued as a criminal matter. He said he would keep it on file for any future problems that may arise in the family. (Case Closed Due to Lack of Evidence) (Case File Information Forwarded to DFYS)

NOTE: *Although I could not pursue this case, I had gained vital information which could be used at a later date, if, in the future, child abuse or neglect did occur. As previously mentioned, I had dealt with Alex on numerous occasions and I knew him to be very volatile when angered. I found he would overreact, due to his inability to control his anger, and it did not take a lot to set him off. Any contact with police seemed to anger him and send him into a rage. Alex was one of my frequent flyers, in that*

I had contact with him often and he was always yelling and threatening anyone he was angry with. He was argumentative on 98% of my contacts with him and I knew him to be very unpredictable. I always was on high alert when dealing with him. Alex will again be mentioned as I tell the stories of my police efforts in, and around, Seldovia.

PROBLEMS IN-HOUSE

On 11/20/91, my day started like most days, during the winters in Seldovia. On this specific day, it was 32 degrees and was cloudy. Snow was in the forecast and it was looking like it could become a reality. I left home and made a pass around town to see that everything was in order and then I went to the office. I had a patrol officer at the time, who I will refer to as 1K-4. He was the nighttime officer, while I covered days. Most investigations had to be done during the daytime hours, so the court system, the district attorney's office, as well as businesses and subjects who were part of an investigation, could be contacted. We had recently come into the digital world and we had been given our first Apple computer. Of course, being somewhat old-school, I was having some difficulty in adjusting. However, 1K-4 had some past experience on a computer and was much more efficient in its use than I. It was my hope we could start typing our police reports on the computer. I found it so much easier to be able to erase, and change your errors, without having to white out, or start the document over, as we had been having to on the typewriter. 1K-4 had shown me how to access the computer and how to use the word program. I was getting better acquainted with it all the time. However, I did not feel comfortable with it yet, so on this morning, I thought I would spend some time getting acquainted better with the computer.

As I was perusing the computer, and the different programs, I came across a letter addressed to the Nissan Vehicle Corporation. The letter was asking that two new Nissan vehicles be donated to the Seldovia Police Department to be used as patrol vehicles. The letter had been written by 1K-4, and signed by him as an officer of the Seldovia Police Department. He referred to the geographical area we served, as being comparable to the size of New Jersey. The letter went on to say we serve a population of approximate 3500 people. Needless to say, the more I read the angrier I became. The officer had taken it on himself to write a letter to Nissan without, first running it past me, but what infuriated me more was the fact he, as an officer of the Seldovia Police Department, would totally fabricate such a story. He literally lied to the organization in an effort to convince them they should donate two vehicles to us. The more I thought about it, the more infuriated I became. I knew myself well enough to know I should not make any important decisions when I was this angry, so I took a different approach. 1K-4 had addressed the letter to a lady in the Nissan organization, who we will call Julie. It was evident the officer had to have done some research, as well, to know who to direct the letter to.

Through directory assistance, I was able to get the telephone number of the Nissan organization in the city where the letter had been addressed. When I asked to speak to Julie, I was transferred to a lady, who came on the phone and ask how she could be of assistance. I told her I was Chief Anderson, of the Seldovia Police Department, and I understand she had received a letter from my patrol officer, and I called 1K-4 by name. I asked her if she knew what letter I was referring to. She said she did and said, in fact she had it lying on her desk at this time. I asked her to read a couple of the paragraphs to me, so there would be no question it was the same letter. Upon her reading the two paragraphs, I found it to be the same correspondence which was on the police department computer. I told Julie the letter was not authorized by me and, even though our vehicles were not in the best shape, we did not serve an area the size of New Jersey, nor do we serve nearly 3500 people. I said, the officer had taken it on his own to write this letter, and without my authorization, and I told her to disregard the letter and I apologized to her for taking up her valuable time.

I now had a dilemma. I was due to go on vacation in a couple weeks and, after this, I didn't feel I could leave 1K-4 in charge. I also didn't know if I could continue to have him as an employee of this police department. I am very emphatic that an Officer be truthful in everything he/she does, with regards to any actions taken in this police department. Had I not found that letter and put a stop to this, I often wondered how 1K-4 would have explained the Nissan Corporation donating two vehicles to the Seldovia Police Department if, in fact, they decided to. I guess he thought the end would justify the means. I don't know how he thought it would not come out, concerning his having lied in the letter. I decided I would talk to 1K-4, before addressing it with the city manager.

I called 1K-4 and asked him if he could come in, a little early, before his shift. He asked what was up and I told him we needed to talk and I would see him at 3:30 PM. By 3:30 PM I had cooled down and was ready to deal with this in a professional manner. 1K-4 showed up and I ask him to have a seat in my office. I told him I had been perusing the computer and I had found a letter, which he had written to the Nissan Corporation. I told him I wanted him to explain in the letter to me. 1K-4 said he was thinking about different ways to get us a couple new vehicles for the department and, since he drove a Nissan, he thought the Nissan would be a good patrol vehicle. He then told me, after some thought, he decided against it and did not send the letter. So, I asked him, "Did you, or did you not, send the letter." 1K-4 looked me straight in the eye, and told me he did not send the letter. I told him that was a blatant lie, because I had talked with a lady named Julie this morning and she assured me the letter was lying on her desk. I told him I asked her to read a couple paragraphs to me. His continuing to lie would only make a bad situation worse, I said. I also told him one cannot have a functioning police department without total honesty. I informed him, I did not know what I was going to do about this, because I could not trust a man who was not totally honest with me. I became even more angry, because he continued to lie to me. I told him I couldn't have a liar working for me. I ordered him to leave the police department now and I told him I will figure out what steps I have to take, because of this. I informed him I would let him know the next day what I had decided. Without another word, 1K-4 stood up and stomped out of the office, noticeably irritated having been caught in more than one obvious lie.

I left the police department and drove to the city offices, where I met with the city manager. I conveyed to him what had taken place and I ask how we should handle the problem. He told me the first thing I had to figure out was, did I want to continue having him in the employ of the city? I told the manager, if we were to terminate 1K-4, my upcoming vacation would have to be put on hold until we could refill the position. I said my tickets were already purchased and my flights were confirmed and I really was not wanting to change anything. I said I was really looking forward to spending Christmas with my family in the states. These plans had been made some time ago and I wondered if there was some other way this could be handled. The city manager said we could give him time off without pay, but that would do nothing more than put the load on me personally. I told the manager I didn't feel we could do anything about the integrity problem anyway, if he would continue to lie to me after being approached, stating he had not mailed the letter. I could not trust anything he said in the future. After more discussion, we decided against giving him time off without pay and would, instead, put a letter of reprimand in his file and put him on a three-month probationary period. The manager said I was to make it very clear to 1K-4, any future problems, dealing with his integrity, would result in his being terminated immediately. We both felt we were only putting off the inevitable, but agreed this is what we had to do given my vacation scheduling problems.

That evening I waited for 1K-4 to come on duty and I called him, via radio, and told him to come to my office. When he arrived, I asked him to have a seat and I told him I had discussed his blatant dishonesty, concerning the letter to Nissan, with the city manager. I told him we had decided we would not terminate him at this time, and we would not be giving him any time off without pay. I went on to tell him, if he displayed any dishonesty, or had any integrity problems at all in the future, it would result in his being terminated immediately.

He was told there would be a letter of reprimand put in his personal file, regarding this matter, and we were placing him on a three-month probationary period. I was very stern with him and told him this type activity would not be tolerated in my police department. I said if the integrity of any member of the police department was compromised, it adversely affected the credibility of the entire police department. The officers of the Seldovia Police Department had to be trusted by the public sector, or we were spinning our wheels. I told him, the more I talked, the angrier I became so, he should leave and go to work, and he best start addressing his integrity problems. 1K-4 never said three words all the time that he was in my office, which was probably the best thing he could've done.

Long story short, I was able to take my three-week vacation, and I visited my family in Florida over the holidays. When I returned, the city manager told me 1K-4 had given his two-week notice and had left the police department. He said he had accumulated enough vacation time, making it possible for him to give his two-week notice and, utilizing his vacation time, he would not have to return to work. Not only had 1K-4 left the police department, he had also left Seldovia. I can honestly say I was not at all disappointed to see him go. Even though I would be the only officer in the department, and have to cover his shift, I was happy to do it just knowing I did not have to worry about a dishonest police officer taking an action that could liable the Seldovia Police Department and the City of Seldovia. We were far better off with no patrol officer at all than we were by having one who was dishonest. How could I trust anything he said in the future?

SEARCH AND RESCUE

It was a cloudy morning and the temperature was 25 degrees, with the southwest wind blowing at approximately 15 miles an hour, when I received a call. At approximately 9:30 AM, the principal at the Susan B. English School, Mike Smith, called and told me he was very concerned about the welfare of the school cook, Cindy Stultz. He said Cindy had not arrived at school yet this morning, and this was totally out of character for her. She always showed up at school around 8:30 AM and started cooking the lunch meal. Mike said she was very conscientious, and anytime she was not able to make it she called in and let him know. He asked if I would do a welfare check on her at her home at 3½ mile, Jakolof Bay Road. I told him I would head out that way immediately and I would let him know what I found out.

I responded to the Stultz residence, which she shared with her boyfriend Donald Huitt. When I arrived, I could find no tracks in the fresh snow, which had fallen on Saturday, 11/7/91. This meant no one had been at the residence Saturday, Sunday, or Monday. Knowing Cindy owned a boat moored in the Seldovia Harbor, the Peter H, I drove back to town to check with the harbor master to see if she and her boyfriend might be out on the boat. Upon reaching the harbor I observed Cindy's truck was parked in the parking lot. I checked with the harbor master, Dan Hecks, and he confirmed Cindy's boat was not in her boat slip. I immediately returned to the police department, where I placed a telephone call to the Homer Harbor Master. I inquired about the vessel, Peter H, and I was told the boat was in the harbor on Sunday night, when the harbor assistant made his rounds. He had listed the Peter H as being on the transient float on Sunday night. The harbor master said the boat was not in the transient area now.

Having gained the information from both the Seldovia and Homer harbor master's, I made a call to the Alaska State Troopers, and talked with Corporal Dan Weatherly. I told him of my findings, and I told him I felt a search & rescue should be organized. Stultz, being so conscientious, and since she had not checked with the school this morning, I felt something was wrong. Corporal Weatherly told me he would check with other harbors if I would go to the Jakolof Bay Harbor and check to see if the boat was moored there. The Corporal also told me to contact him, via radio, as to my findings and, if necessary, he would alert the Coast Guard. After getting off the phone with the trooper, I immediately called Mike Smith at the school and told him what was taking place. I conveyed this to Mike because he had to call someone in to cook lunch for the students and, also because he was concerned about Stultz's welfare.

I traveled to Jakolof Bay Harbor but found no trace of the Peter H so I returned to Seldovia. In route I called Corporal Weatherly, via radio, and advised him I did not locate the boat. He said he would call the Coast Guard and give them all the information we had up to this point. Corporal Weatherly also called Larry Thompson, owner/operator of Homer Air Service, and asked if he would check the Kachemak Bay area in his travels to and from Seldovia.

At approximately 12:45 PM, Larry Thompson called and asked that I come out to the Seldovia airport. When I met with him, he told me he had spotted some boat debris, which resembled the canopy, portholes and the stern section off the Peter H. He said it was located on the east side of Hesketh Island, just north of the old Doglish home. He said he also had spotted other debris which, appeared to be, plastic and a red door, the same color door which was on the Peter H. He told me these were observed on the beach at Yukon Island. I immediately relayed the information to Corporal Weatherly at AST in Homer and he said he would let the Coast Guard know. The trooper also said the

Coast Guard was sending a helicopter out of Kodiak and an inflatable out of Homer to assist in the search.

Thompson left Seldovia, and after a short time, returned. I was again summoned to the airport and met with him. He told me, upon leaving Seldovia, he had observed, what appeared to be a survival suit floating face down. He said the survival suit was located just off the rocky point at Barabara Point. He told me couldn't be sure if a body was in the survival suit because it was floating face down. He said he had returned to Seldovia to meet with me so he would not have to put this information over the radio. I immediately called Corporal Weatherly, by telephone, and relayed Thompson's sightings to him. Corporal Weatherly said he would advise the Coast Guard.

At approximately 1530 hours Corporal Weatherly arrived at the Seldovia airport, where I met with him and provided transportation to the Seldovia PD. Upon entering the police department, I received a call from Doctor Larry Reynolds, Seldovia's resident doctor. Doctor Reynolds told me he was at the Homer hospital when the Coast Guard brought a body in. He said he identified the body as being that of Cindy Stultz and he said he was the one who pronounced her deceased. He said she was floating face down in a survival suit when she was found. Doctor Reynolds was her attending physician, so there was no question as to her identity.

Approximately one hour later, Corporal Weatherly received a call reporting Donald Huitt's body had also been located, and he was also deceased. His body was found on the rocks on the southeast end of Hesketh Island. He was not in a survival suit, but a suit was found near him. It had never been taken out of its bag.

Even though the two bodies had been recovered, the case was not closed at that point. The police needed to locate, and notify, the next of kin of both the victims, and hopefully reveal the reason for the boat's sinking. The two victims had no relatives in the Seldovia area but Corporal Weatherly did gain information Cindy Stultz's had relatives in, or around, Plano, Texas. The Corporal forwarded this information to dispatch, and asked them to look into it. Corporal Weatherly and I then responded to the Stultz residence to check for any paperwork which might point us toward any relatives of Donald Huitt's. Upon searching the residence, we found a paper with the last name of Huitt on it. When exiting the home, we sealed the residence with police barricade tape. This hopefully would deter any undesirables from entering.

On 12/10/91, Magistrate Coughenower, of the Homer Court, flew to Seldovia to take inventory of the items at the Stultz residence, since there was no next of kin in the area to release the property to. The inventory was taken and there were six cats found inside the residence. They were delivered to a lady in town who agreed to see to their welfare. The Magistrate instructed me to buy 25 pounds of kitty litter for the lady, and to charge it to the court system. A number of different pieces of jewelry were also taken by the Magistrate, and would be placed in safekeeping. Some eagle feathers, found at the residence, were confiscated. Upon exiting the residence, the police barricade tape was again placed across the entrance to seal the residence. The Magistrate was then returned to the airport where, at approximately 4:30 PM, she boarded her flight back to Homer, taking the items which were collected with her.

The Peter H was described as 38-foot harbor tug, powered by a single diesel engine. It had a 10½ foot beam, *width from side to side,* with a substructure, the cabin, being red and white in color and was a wooden vessel. The hall was reportedly painted black. The boat had an after deck, *the back deck of the vessel,* said to be approximately 10-foot-long, with a tow bit located near the aft, *rear,* bulkhead of the pilothouse. There was a deck awning, *or covering*, which protruded out approximately six feet aft of the wheelhouse. The boat was built in San Francisco in 1926.

After calling the police department in Plano, Texas, Corporal Weatherly was contacted by a brother of Cindy Stultz's. He told the trooper he had just been advised of his sister's death. He said her mother and father lived in Mineola, Texas and he would be talking to them as soon as he gained some more information from Trooper Weatherly. He asked some cursory questions regarding the cause of the boat sinking and if Donald Huitt was with her at the time. After having all his questions answered, the conversation was terminated.

On 12/11/91, at approximately 7:10 AM, Corporal Weatherly received a phone call from Dorothy Stultz, the mother of Cindy Stultz. She informed the trooper, Cindy's father's name was John Stultz, and they lived in Mineola, Texas. Mrs. Stultz asked what responsibility they would have, reference her daughter's estate. Corporal Weatherly gave her the number to the Homer Court and asked she call Magistrate Coughenower, the coroner handling this case. He told her the Magistrate could answer any questions she might have in that regard. Mrs. Stultz also stated she had talked to her daughter, approximately three weeks ago, and she told her then they were planning a trip to Homer for Christmas shopping on this past weekend. She thanked Corporal Weatherly for the information and told him she would be contacting the Magistrate after 8:00 AM, Alaska time. The trooper gave his condolences and they ended the conversation.

In locating the next of kin for Donald Huitt, Corporal Weatherly found it to be a daunting task. He had followed up two or three leads which had been dead ends. He was contacted by Homer dispatch and told of a possible step-son of Donald Huitt's, who was said to live in the Portland, Oregon area. However, dispatch could not find a telephone number or a physical address for the 27-year-old, so there was no way to contact him. Further investigation led to information that Donald Huitt had four or five siblings, two which were reportedly deceased, leaving three others still living. No one had any idea where they resided so that information was of no help either.

After some research, a brother was alleged to live in White Salmon, Washington, but no telephone number was listed. Corporal Weatherly called the police department in White Salmon and they said White Salmon was a small town and none of the officers there knew the person said to be Huitt's brother. They checked for any Huitt's listed using the utilities of the city and none could be found. They even checked with the post master and he did not recognize anyone with the name Huitt as having received any mail.

Corporal Weatherly kept attempting to locate the next of kin for Huitt and, through his investigation, he found an ex-wife alleged to be living in Ketchikan. There was no telephone listing so the Corporal called the Alaska State Trooper post in Ketchikan and talked with Trooper Edmondson. Upon Trooper Edmondson being advised there was possibly an ex-wife in Ketchikan, he said he would check it out and get back to Corporal Weatherly as soon as possible. At approximately 4:33 PM, Trooper Edmondson called Corporal Weatherly and told him he had located Huitt's ex-wife and was with her at that time. The ex-wife was given the phone and talked directly with Corporal Weatherly. She told the Corporal, Donald Huitt was a Klamath/Modoc Indian, from the Southern Oregon area. She said they had been divorced for over five years. She told the trooper Huitt also had taken another last name of Switlick. He had been in a foster home with a family whose last name was Switlick, and when he was in his mid-20's, he took that as his last name. She suggested the trooper's attempt to contact the Bureau of Indian affairs in Klamath, Oregon. She said she had lost all track of him, upon leaving Homer, and didn't know where any of his family were at this time.

As suggested by Huitt's ex-wife, Corporal Weatherly called the Bureau of Indian affairs and, after some searching, they did find they had a member of the tribe with the name listed as Donald Switlick and he had the same date of birth as Donald Huitt. They said they could not determine if it was one in the same. They told the trooper they would do some research and would call him later in the day. Possibly three hours later the trooper was called by a lady, identifying herself as the mother of Donald Huitt, a.k.a. Donald Switlick. She told the officer she was from Klamath Falls, Oregon. The lady went on to tell the trooper she would like the deceased's fingerprints taken to make a positive identification that it was, in fact, her son who had drowned. She told Corporal Weatherly, she did not have any wish to have the remains sent to Oregon and further, she did not feel the Klamath/Modoc tribe would want his remains either. She did want the trooper to call her, following the fingerprint identification, and let her know if it was indeed her son. The trooper was not given any reason why the woman wouldn't want the remains shipped to them, but he came to the conclusion, there had to have been something bad happen in Huitt's past which made him somewhat of an outcast with his family.

The fingerprints were taken of the deseased and a positive identification was made of Donald Huitt. Corporal Weatherly called the mother back and shared the findings with her.

Two separate boat operators were contacted, who had been commercial fishing in Kachemak Bay, off of Barabara point, on the day of the drownings. Both captains said they were acquainted with the tug, Peter H. They both said the weather, on the day in question, was blowing Southwest at approximately 30 to 35 mile per hour. They estimated the seas were 12 to 15 feet and both captains had observed the Peter H headed in the direction of Seldovia, bucking hard into the seas. One of the captains said every time the boat would crest the wave you could see most of it's keel. Both agreed the tug was in poor condition and should never have been bucking into that heavy of a sea. They felt the boat should have never left Homer Harbor, with the forecast being what it was. One captain stated he thought they most probably tried to turn around and were hit by a wave, and rolled over. In reality, it's impossible to speculate as to what did actually happen, but two people lost their lives, and it was most probably due to lack of experience on the water.

Cindy Stultz and Donald Huitt were well liked in, and around, Seldovia. The loss of their lives was very impacting to the citizens of our town. They had spoken about turning the Peter H into a commercial enterprise. We, the people that knew them, still miss them and we still talk about them ever so often. (Case closed by investigation)

Assault 4th Degree/Misconduct Involving Weapons 3rd Degree

I t was raining and the temperature was around 35 degrees on January 5, 1992, when I heard a knock on my front door at around 10:30 PM. Upon answering the door, I found a lady and her daughter to be soaking wet, and it was evident the lady had been crying. I knew them both and I asked them to step inside out of the weather and then I inquired what was going on. The lady told me her husband, a good friend of mine, had come home intoxicated and they had gotten into an argument and he had assaulted her. She said the argument started because her husband was not happy with the dinner she had cooked. She said he started hitting her in the face, on the head and on her back, with his fist. I observed her to have marks on her forehead, resembling scratches, and I further observed her face to be swollen and there was a skinned area on her right cheek, close to her nose. The subject was shaking, very distraught, and on the verge of tears. It was evident her daughter had also been crying. I inquired if the daughter had been assaulted and she told me no, he had not hit her. The daughter said she was in the bathroom and heard her mother screams and she ran out of the bathroom and ran to the bedroom, where she observed her father hit her mother twice in the back. She said she ran over and hit her father in the head with her hand, pulled him off of her mother, and yelled for her mother to run. Together they ran out of the house and came to my residence for help. The victim had run out of her home without any shoes and had to walk through the snow to my house in her stocking feet. She told me she didn't have time to grab her shoes. I inquired if the victim needed medical assistance and she said not at that time, but she was starting to get a headache.

My wife, Ann, had not gone to bed yet and I asked her to make the victim and her daughter comfortable until I could make contact with her husband. I told the victim she and her daughter would be safe at my home and my wife had a radio, so she could contact me if, for some reason, her husband came to my house before I had contact with him.

I then responded to the suspect's residence. Since the suspect and I had worked together on a commercial king crab fishing vessel a few years previously, and were very well acquainted, I felt I could talk him down and be able to resolve this without any further violence. Upon arrival at the suspect's residence, I observed the lights had been shut off and the house was dark. When I knocked on the door no one would answer. I called my wife on my radio and had her inquire of the victim if there were any keys available so I could access the residence. I was told the keys were in the victim's purse inside her residence, but she said the back door to the residence was usually unlocked. I trudged through the nearly 3 feet of snow, to the back door, and found it was indeed unlocked. I opened the door and called out, identifying myself, and told the suspect I needed to talk to him. He yelled back and told me he had a .357 caliber Smith & Wesson revolver and he was loading it and I was not to enter his home without a warrant. I continued my attempt to communicate with him, but he told me to get out right now, and he then fired the weapon. I didn't think he was shooting at me and he, most probably, fired into the ceiling or the floor, to discourage any entry. However, I immediately told him I was backing off, but I also told him I was not going to go away. I was only a foot or so inside the residence but I quickly backed off and closed the door. Even though I knew the suspect very well, I was not sure what he would do in his intoxicated state, so I backed out and closed the door.

I trudged through the deep snow to the northwest of the home, where I could see the front door. I then yelled to the suspect, trying to persuade him to come out before he made matters much worse than they had to be. After approximately 15 to 20 minutes of negotiations, yelling back and forth, I was finally able to persuade the suspect to put his weapon down and exit the front door. I instructed him to keep his hands in front of him at all times, to ensure he had no weapons. The subject said he was afraid the police would shoot him. I told the suspect that he knew me and he knew I was not going to hurt him, if he complied with my demands. I told him to come out and to keep his hands where I could see them at all times. He finally yelled to me that he was coming out and not to shoot. I instructed him to put both hands out the door, to show me he was not armed, and with his arms outstretched, I then told him to walk on out of the door. I directed him to face away from me and to go down onto his knees. I then told him to put his hands on his head, interlock his fingers, and not to move. After having to repeat my directions a couple times, he finally did as I requested. I approached him, holstered my weapon, and then placed him in handcuffs. I patted him down for weapons and, finding none, I placed him in the front passenger seat of my patrol vehicle. I transported the suspect to the Seldovia Police Department and, due to his degree of intoxication, he was immediately put through the booking process and placed in the jail cell. He would be given an opportunity to tell his side of the story, in the morning, when he sobered up if he chose to.

Upon entry to the police department, I called my wife and told her I had the suspect in custody and it was safe for the victim and her daughter to go home. I also told my wife to tell her I would need to interview her if she could come to the police department in approximately an hour. Ann told me she would relay the information to her and I hung up.

At approximately 11:53 PM I interviewed the victim at the police department and the conversation was tape recorded. The victim said it was after 10:00 PM when her husband came home from the bar intoxicated. She said he told her he wanted something to eat and for her to fix it. She said she fixed him something to eat and then, a short time later, he became angry, telling her he didn't like what she had to fixed him to eat. She said he then started hitting her with his fist in the head, face, and on the back, knocking her down on the bed in their bedroom. She said she rolled over to avoid being hit in the face and he continued to hit her in the back. Her daughter, who had been in the bathroom, came out and hit her father, then pulled him off of her. She said she heard her daughter yell, telling her to run, and she bolted out the front door. She said her daughter ran out of the house with her and together they ran to my house. The victim stated she didn›t have time to get her shoes so she ran through the snow in her stocking feet. She also told me, she had been assaulted by her husband in October of this year, in the parking lot at the clinic. He was not intoxicated that time, she said, and he had banged her head against the car, and she had to have three stitches due to a cut on her head.

Following the interview, I encouraged the victim to get a Temporary Restraining Order, (TRO), to keep her husband from being able to return to the residence until this matter was over. I assisted her in filling out the paperwork. I then faxed the forms to the court system. I wrote a note on the face of the fax transmittal sheet, asking that they address the issue before the suspect got out of jail the following morning.

The victim said she was suffering from a headache, resulting from the assault. I encouraged her to seek medical attention and told her I would call the doctor, if she didn't object. She agreed and I called Doctor Larry Reynolds of the Seldovia clinic. He was home and would have to travel to town, so he said he would come to the police department, pick up the victim, and escort her to the clinic. Prior to her leaving with the doctor, I asked that she sign a release of information form at the doctor's office, so he could release his findings to the police. I also asked if she could contact her daughter and have her come in for an interview, if it wasn't too late for her.

At approximately 12:11 AM, 1/6/92, I interviewed the daughter of the victim at my office and the interview was tape recorded. I asked her to tell me what had occurred and she told me her father had come home intoxicated but, she said, he was acting differently than he usually did when he was drunk. She said he was much more talkative than usual. She told me she had gone into the bathroom and heard her father walk down the hall to the bedroom, where her mother was.

She said, the next thing she heard was her mother telling her father to get away from her. She said she exited the bathroom and headed for the living room, where she was going to call the police for assistance, but her mother was yelling for help so she ran into the bedroom. She observed her father hitting her mother in the back twice, but said she knows her mother was hit more times than that before she left the bathroom. She continued, stating she ran to them and hit her father in the head with her fist and pulled him off of her mother. She then yelled for her mother to run and she ran with her. They ran through the snow to my home to get help. She said that was all she could remember that took place.

A jail guard had been called and had arrived to guard the prisoner overnight. I left the police department, after interviewing the daughter, and I went to the victim's residence and secured two .357 caliber revolvers, their holsters and ammunition. I took the weapon's and placed them in safekeeping in the evidence locker at the police department. It would be up to the court whether or not the suspect would be able to retrieve the weapons when this was all over.

The following morning, upon reaching the police department, I found the TRO had been ordered and had been faxed to the police department, to be served on the suspect. I brought the suspect out of the jail cell and served him with the TRO. I then read him his Miranda rights warning. He stated he wanted to contact an attorney before signing anything. I allowed him to make numerous calls in his attempts to contact an attorney. Finally, he was able to reach a lawyer in Homer. Through his attorney the court was contacted and released the suspect, pending arraignment, on his own recognizance with certain restrictions. The suspect was required to sign a document agreeing to abstain from any consumption of alcohol and not to enter any establishment whose main purpose was the sale of alcohol. The subject did sign the agreement and was released on his own recognizance.

Upon his release the suspect requested I accompany him to his residence, so he could pick up some needed items. He said he would move onto his boat. As per his request, I did accompany him to his residence and he did gather up what he would need during his absence from his home. Prior to leaving the home, he asked what weapons I had confiscated. I told him I had confiscated two .357 caliber pistols, their holsters, and some ammunition. At that point, he raised the end of the couch in the living room area, and I observed a pistol lying on the rug. He told me that was the pistol he had shot into the floor on the night in question. I picked it up, and checked to see if it was loaded, and found one round had been fired. There was only one spent cartridge in the weapon. The suspect told me he had fired it into the floor of the residence when I was at the back door. I took that weapon as evidence and we exited the residence. I delivered the suspect to the boat harbor with his personal belongings and then returned to the police department. I logged the .357 in the evidence, and placed it in the evidence locker.

The suspect, through his attorney, pled not guilty to the charges of Assault in the 4Th Degree and Misconduct Involving Weapons in the 3rd Degree, both "A" class misdemeanors. Trial was set for a later date.

As in most cases, the suspect's attorney and the district attorney got together and a plea bargain was reached. No trial would take place if the suspect would plead to the assault on his wife. They agreed to drop the misconduct involving weapons charges.

Since the suspect did not have any prior criminal violations, he was sentenced to 30 days in jail with 30 days suspended and given a $500 fine with $250 suspended. He was further told to report to the South Kachemak Inc. Alcoholism Program, (SKIAP), and undertake alcohol screening and to comply with their recommendations. He was placed on probation for two years wherein he was to have no criminal violations. (Case closed by arrest)

NOTE: *The suspect, in this case, was a personal friend of mine, which made it somewhat difficult for me to investigate. However, I was a police officer, and I had sworn I would protect the public, regardless of the circumstances. When I was dealing with a personal friend, I always tried to think of them as if they were strangers. I attempted to deal with all violations and crimes in a professional manner, regardless of who I was dealing with. At times like this, it would have been considerably less stressful if I could have handed the case off to some other officer and just walked away, however this was not possible. All I could do was deal with the matter as professionally as possible, and with respect for my friend, regardless of the circumstances and regardless of the outcome.*

Assault in the 4th Degree

When I left for work on the morning of 2/21/92, it was +18 degrees and it was snowing. The day consisted of a number of animal control calls and a couple assistance requests but, other than that, I spent the day catching up on paperwork and fielding phone calls. Following my shift, I headed home to relax and have dinner. At approximately 6:43 PM, the police phone rang at my home and, upon answering, I was told by a concerned citizen, there was a fight was in progress outside the Knight Spot Bar on Main Street, and the police were needed. I told my wife to keep dinner warm and I would be back as soon as possible. As always, neither of us knew when that would be.

I geared up quickly and responded to the Knight Spot Bar. Upon arrival I observed Tommy, our local problem child, and his father in a heated argument. I exited my vehicle and yelled for them to break it up. Before I could reach them to separate them, Tommy hit his father full in the face with a right-handed roundhouse. Tommy's father was knocked to the ground. I immediately put Tommy into the wall face first, telling him he was under arrest for assault in the 4th degree. Tommy was yelling, stating his father had started the fight and he was only defending himself. I told Tommy, when I came on the scene and told him to quit, he ignored me and hit his father in my presence. He said he didn't know I was there and his father had punched him first. I told him I had not witnessed his father swing on him but I

195

had witnessed him hit his father after I told him to stop. I patted him down for weapons and then, finding no weapons, I turned him around, walking him to my police vehicle.

A crowd had gathered and had helped Tommy's father to his feet. I asked him if he needed medical assistance and he stated he was fine, but said it was a good thing I was arresting his son because if I hadn't come along when I did, there would have been hell to pay. I told Tommy's father, I would take it from here and for him to chill out. I did observe his lower lip to be split and I saw blood on it. I told him I would want to talk to him about what happened later, but I would contact him at another time. He said he'd be around and he headed back into the Knight Spot.

Tommy had a strong odor of alcohol on his breath and his voice was slurred. His eyes were bloodshot and his cheeks were flushed. As in every case with Tommy, when he was approached, while under the influence of alcohol, he was argumentative, threatening, and combative. His threatening statements and his never-ending insults only tend to prove he is under the influence of alcohol. When contacted without any alcohol aboard, Tommy was, usually, pretty easy to communicate with.

I transported Tommy to the Seldovia Police Department where, after starting the voice recorder, I read him his Miranda warning. He kept interrupting and told me he wasn't answering any questions. He said he wanted an attorney. Every time I would start to say something Tommy would interrupt, and start talking, making it very hard to communicate. Tommy insisted his father had hit him first and he was only defending himself. I did observe a swelling on the left side of Tommy's face, as well as some scratches on his left cheek. I took two photographs of the injuries.

As, on a number of previous occasions, I photographed him and put him through the booking process. I then locked him in the cell. Immediately after locking him in the cell, Tommy demanded I give him his one telephone call. I brought him out of the cell and let him make his phone call. He called his captain of the boat he was fishing on and, after a time, his captain came to the police department with

$500 cash, to bail Tommy out. I told Tommy, along with the bail of $500, he would have to sign a release form, agreeing he would not consume alcoholic beverages or enter any establishment whose main purpose was the sale of alcoholic beverages. I informed him this would stay in effect until he went before the court and there was a disposition in this case. Even though he was unhappy about the requirements, he did sign the release form. I then released him into the custody of his captain, informing him he was not to be around his father.

After I released Tommy, I drove to the Knight Spot bar and contacted his father. I brought him out of the bar and interviewed him in the police vehicle. He told me he and his son had gotten into an argument inside the bar and had gone outside just prior to my arrival. He said, at no time, did he hit his son, but said his son did hit him in the face. When I asked him what they were arguing about, he told me it had to do with the family matter and that's all he would say. Even though he was drinking, he was not to the point of impairment, in my opinion. He did smell of alcohol, and his eyes were bloodshot but his voice was not slurred and he was steady on his feet. I observed his lip to be very swollen and look to be very painful. I told him I could call in medical assistance if he felt he needed it, but he declined any medical assistance.

Tommy showed up for arraignment, at the Homer court, and pled not guilty to the charge of assault in the 4th degree. The case was set over for trial and Tommy was informed he was still under the requirements of his release. He was told he could not enter any bar or consume any intoxicating liquor, and was to have no contact with his father.

Approximately 2 weeks had passed since Tommy's arraignment, when he contacted the court and requested a change of plea hearing. At the change of plea hearing, Tommy pled guilty to the charge of assault in the 4th degree and he was sentenced to 100 days in jail with 100 days suspended, a $500 fine with $250 suspended, he was placed on probation for 2 years wherein he could have no criminal offenses and he was given 30 hours of community service to be performed for the city of Seldovia. He was given 3 months in which to complete the community service. (Case closed by arrest)

NOTE: *As in past cases, I was again dissatisfied with the decisions by the court. Even though Tommy had a very lengthy criminal record, he was still given a very light sentence. I feel, when a person is told to stop a criminal activity by a police officer, and they fail to do so, and the activity constitutes a criminal act, their actions should aggravate any sentencing they receive, resulting from their guilty plea. In Tommy's case, they didn't even order alcohol screening. However, I did what I could do as a police officer, and since I'm not a judge, I guess I shouldn't be critiquing their actions, regardless of how frustrating it is.*

DWI, DRIVING WHILE LICENSE SUSPENDED & MICS 6TH DEGREE

On 7/20/92, we had enjoyed a beautiful day in Seldovia. Temperature was 60°, and the sun was shining with clear skies and the wife and I had been invited to Corky and Carol Myers home for dinner. Following a great meal, we were sitting around visiting, when my radio/telephone rang at approximately 7:52 PM. When I answered, Homer police dispatch told me they had received a call of a van over the embankment on Kachemak Drive. The caller also told them the door of the vehicle had hung up on a tree, keeping the vehicle from going into the Seldovia Slough. The caller did not know if there were any injuries in the accident.

Corky Myers asked me if he could accompany me and he and I responded to the location. In responding, I found the vehicle was over the embankment on Bay Street, not Kachemak Drive. We were the first to arrive on scene and I called the Fire/EMT dispatch, making them aware of the correct location. The vehicle had gone over the embankment backwards, and the driver's door, which had to have been open, was hung up on a tree, stopping the vehicle from going further over the embankment and, possibly, into the Seldovia Slough. I observed a man sitting on the ground near the rear driver-side tire, and he was complaining about having pain to his lower leg and ankle. Gasoline was dripping from the vehicle and in close proximity to the injured man.

The EMTs and fire department had not yet arrived on scene, so I went down over the embankment to the injured man. I asked him what happened and he said he was attempting to park the vehicle on the incline, across Bay Street, and was exiting the vehicle when it started rolling backwards. He said he attempted to reenter the vehicle and stop it, but was he had been struck by the tree the door had hung up on. I smelled a strong odor of alcohol when talking to the man and I observed his speech to be very slurred. It appeared he was having a hard time focusing his eyes and I suspected he was highly intoxicated. I pulled him away from the vehicle and the dripping gasoline, so he would be safe if the vehicle moved or a fire started.

The EMTs and fire department arrived on the scene and I left the patient to them and I informed the fire department of the leaking gas. I continued to my police vehicle and readied my portable breath test instrument. When EMTs brought the man up next to the ambulance, on the stretcher, I asked him to give me a breath sample and, to my surprise, he complied. The breath test resulted in a blood alcohol reading of .261. The EMTs treated the man and transported him to the Seldovia clinic, to be seen by Doctor Larry Reynolds.

Due to the gas leak, I informed the fire department personnel, I was going to call a local contractor, Jim Hopkins, of Hopkins Brothers Construction, and have him remove the vehicle from the embankment. The Fire Chief was in total agreement and said it was a fire hazard the way it was positioned and steps did need to be taken to alleviate that hazard. Upon calling Mr. Hopkins, I was told he would be there in approximately 30 minutes, to remove the vehicle. I told the Fire Chief if he needed me to call on the radio, because I was going to see if I could locate the owner of the van, and I left the scene.

I was acquainted with the owner of the blue van and I went to the Knight Spot bar in an effort to locate him. Upon finding him, I asked him to come outside where I could talk to him. I told him what had taken place and he told me he had not given the man permission to take his vehicle. The owner told me the vehicle had been parked at the Knight Spot bar before it was taken. I asked him if he wanted to report it stolen and he said no, because the man worked for him and he most likely assumed he had permission to drive it. The owner asked me how much damage the van had sustained and I told him the driver's door would most probably have to be replaced but I didn't observe any other serious damage. While I was with the owner of the van, I received a telephone call from Jim Hopkins, stating he wanted a release of liability waiver signed by the owner, before he would remove the vehicle. He said, he wasn't going to take the chance of having to pay for any damage that might be sustained in the removal of the vehicle. At that point I wrote out a waiver, which I felt would hold up in court, and the owner signed it. I then left and delivered the waiver to Mr. Hopkins.

Mr. Hopkins was in agreement with the waiver and the vehicle was removed from the embankment and placed in the owner's driveway with Mr. Hopkins boom truck.

Prior to the vehicle being removed, using my 35 mm Canon camera, I took pictures of the vehicle and of the area. I also took pictures of the vehicle when it was being removed and after its removal from the embankment.

Upon his being released by Doctor Reynolds, I arrested the driver, who had been operating the van, and charged him with the DWI. His ankle had not been broken and he was able to walk on it, so I walked him to the police department. Upon arrival at the police department, I patted them down and found a marijuana pipe in his right front pocket. A check of the residue in the pipe resulted in a positive reading for the presence of THC. I then charged him with misconduct involving a controlled substance in the 6th degree. After reading him is Miranda warning, the subject stated he was not going to admit to driving while intoxicated, in that he had only moved the vehicle into the driveway and had tried to stop it when it started rolling backwards. He refused to sign his waiver. After having observed the subject without anything in his mouth for a period of 25 minutes, I administered the Intoximeter breath test, which resulted in a finding of .256 blood alcohol content.

The subject was photographed and booked and then placed in the holding cell. A jail guard was called to watch over the suspect until he could be brought before the court at arraignment.

A subsequent background check resulted in finding the man to be operating the vehicle after his license had been revoked. Due to this he was also charged with driving while license revoked.(DWLR) I informed him of all the charges I would be bringing and I told him, unless he can make bail, he would be held until 1:30 PM tomorrow when he would be arraigned telephonically from the police department. He was unable to make bail so he was held until arraignment the next afternoon.

At arraignment the subject pled no contest on the charge of driving while intoxicated and he was sentenced to a $500 fine with $250 suspended, he was ordered to serve 40 days in jail with all but 72 hours suspended, his license was revoked for 90 days, he was ordered to report to the SKIAP alcohol program and undergo alcohol screening and he was to pay all related fees. He was placed on probation for 2 years wherein he was ordered to commit no criminal violations.

On the charge of DWLR, the subject pled no contest and was fined $500 with $200 suspended, was ordered to serve 30 days in jail with 20 days suspended, to be completed by 8/15/92 and his operator's license was revoked for 90 days, concurrent with previous court actions, and he was to surrender his driver's license to the court immediately.

On the charges of misconduct involving a controlled substance in the 6th degree, the defendant pled no contest and was sentenced to a fine of $100 with $0 suspended and was placed on probation for two years wherein he was to commit no criminal violations.

Following arraignment, the subject was given his personal belongings, minus the pot pipe, and was released. (Case closed by arrest)

A WEDDING CEREMONY, TAKEN TO NEW HEIGHTS

It was December 1992, when I received a phone call from Larry Thompson, owner/operator of Homer Air Service. He told me he was getting married on the 12th day of December and he wanted to personally invite me to his wedding. I told him it was about time he was tying the knot and I'd be glad to come. He said he wanted to see if I would consider being his best man. It would be a gross understatement were I to say I was humbled by this. I certainly would never say no, feeling honored as I did, but it did catch me off guard. Larry and I had been friends for many years and I always respected him and had the highest admiration regarding his abilities when flying an airplane. He was one of those pilots, who we refer to, as someone who doesn't get into an airplane, he puts the airplane on. In other words, it's as if they become part of the aircraft they are piloting. There are only a couple other pilots I've ever flown with who I would put in the same category as Larry Thompson. They were two other close friends, Bob Gruber, owner/operator of Cook Inlet Aviation, and Jack Hines, a pilot who actually flew commercially for both Bob and Larry, at different times.

After I told him I would be honored to be his best man, Larry told me he would have an airplane pick me up at 10:00 AM on the morning of the 12th, and transport me to Homer. When I ask if I should wear a suit and tie, or a tuxedo, Thompson laughed, and told me this was going to be a very casual affair. He said they were going to get married in an airplane. Of course, I thought he was jerking me around but, knowing him as I did, I should not have been at all surprised. With his whole life being all about airplanes, plus owning his own charter airlines, I should have known he would work an airplane into the deal somehow. He said for me to show up at 10:00 AM, at the Seldovia airport, and he would fill me in on the rest later. He did ask if it would be possible to find a place to have the wedding reception in Seldovia. I told him I didn't think it would be a problem, and I offered to check to see if we could get the multipurpose room from the city for the event. Larry then asked if my wife, Ann, could round up a few of her girlfriends and set everything up for the wedding reception. I told him I couldn't really speak for my wife, but I would ask her and let him know.

Of course, when I asked my wife, she readily agreed to do whatever was needed. She called Dianne Gruber and asked for her assistance and Dianne quickly agreed to help out. I called the city and found the multipurpose room was available on that date and it was set aside for the event. Ann and Dianne took the reins and started planning what would be needed to pull this off. Now the only thing left for me was to show up at the Seldovia airport at 10:00 AM on Saturday morning.

I arrived a few minutes early on December 12th, and at 10:00 AM, Ken Day, the pilot for Homer Air, picked myself and one other passenger up and flew us to Homer. Upon reaching Homer, I went into the Homer Airlines office and found Larry and Dee, his fiancée, putting things together which would be needed in their wedding. I thought it was a little strange the two would be there together. Not at all what you would call traditional. The bride wasn't supposed to even see the groom before the ceremony. I was about to find out how far from a traditional ceremony this wedding was going to be.

Larry greeted me and told me what they had planned. He said they were going to be married in the skies over Seldovia. He said we were going to take the Islander, a twin-engine, eight seated aircraft, with myself, a photographer, the Magistrate, the bridesmaid, Dee and himself aboard, and we were going to fly to Seldovia. Upon reaching the Seldovia area, we would circle town while the Magistrate performed the wedding ceremony. He said I would be setting in the back seat of the airplane and beside me would be a cooler, which contained some champagne and champagne glasses. Following the Magistrate pronouncing them man and wife, I would pour each of us a glass of champagne, other than the pilot of course, and we would then toast the newlyweds. Following the toast, we would land and then proceed to the multipurpose room for the reception.

Even after Larry had lined me out, it was still only 10:45 AM, and the reception was set to start at 1:00 PM. We had a little time to kill before we needed to take off. The plan was for us to be ready to fly by noon, which would give us ample time to fly to Seldovia, perform the ceremony and be at the multipurpose room by 1:00 PM.

At high noon we taxied out and took off, with Ken Day piloting the aircraft. Sitting in the copilot seat was the photographer, who had been hired to videotape the ceremony. In the second seat, Magistrate Coughenower and the bridesmaid, Patty Morris, were seated, with Larry and Dee taking up the third seat. As aforementioned, I and a cooler, took up the rear seat of the airplane. Each of us aboard had a headset, with mics attached, so everyone could hear what was going on, as well as communicate, if needed. A voice recorder had also been wired into the headsets so the ceremony could be audio taped as well as videotaped. It seemed they had covered all the bases and the only thing left was for the Magistrate to tie the knot. (*Tie the knot always reminded me of readying a rope for a hanging. I'm glad it meant something different for this type occasion.*)

We arrived in the skies over Seldovia and Ken started circling the town. It appeared we were 1500 to 2000 feet in altitude. The photographer had turned half way around in his seat and was videotaping as Magistrate Coughenower performed the ceremony. As soon as the Magistrate pronounced them husband-and-wife, and they had kissed, I popped the top on the champagne bottle, without blowing a hole in the aircraft. I poured the champagne, one goblet at a time, then pasted each of them forward. After everyone had their glass in hand, we congratulated and toasted the new bride and groom. Mr. Day then landed the aircraft and, with transportation being already pre-arranged, everyone headed to the multipurpose room. The married couple took up the second seat in my patrol vehicle. The pilot drove the Homer Airlines courtesy car into town and our local taxi provided transportation for the rest of the crew.

Everyone in town had been made aware of the wedding and all were invited to the reception. When we arrived, it appeared most of the town's population was there. Ann and Dianne had done an outstanding job, as usual, and the reception came off without a hitch. Having not been involved in that part of the preparation, I don't know who baked the cake and supplied all the food, but there was certainly enough to go around. I'm sure everyone in town would want to do what they could for Larry and Dee. Larry had been such a huge part of the community for so many years and he was loved by everyone. Because Dee was now his wife, she too, was welcomed with open arms. The reception lasted most of the afternoon, with everyone wanting to congratulate the newly married couple. Larry had made arrangements to spend the night at the Boardwalk Hotel. I'm not sure who had the idea, or who all was involved, but somehow, someone got in to the newlywed's room, and short-sheeted their bed. When I found out about that, I thought it was hilarious and only wished I could have been able to take part in it.

On Sunday morning, December 13th, the weather had turned, and it was snowing. No planes were flying and, during the winter in Seldovia, very few businesses were open and, no businesses were open on Sunday. Larry and Dee were somewhat stranded, with no way to leave town and nothing open, where they could get a meal. Ann and I took pity on them and had them over to the house where we visited, chowed up and had a great afternoon. They returned to the Boardwalk Hotel for another night and, come Monday morning, it had cleared enough so they could fly back to Homer, to their home.

At the time of this writing Larry and Dee will be celebrating their twenty-eighth wedding anniversary in December. Even though Larry has retired and sold Homer Airlines, we still stay in touch. Larry spends his summers in Homer, where he keeps an airplane so he can visit all his friends on this side of the Bay. Larry and Dee spend their winters in Arizona where they enjoy the warmer climate. Last year, 2019, they drove to Alaska from Arizona, in their motorhome, and stayed the summer. We had a great visit and, I thoroughly enjoyed seeing Larry and Dee again. In the fall they drove back from Homer to Arizona, where they now reside. I guess you could say, they've become snowbirds. That was something I never thought Thompson would do but, he seems to enjoy it and, it has now become his way of life. That warm weather probably feels really good on his old bones. He does seem anxious to get back to Alaska every spring, though. I'm sure this lifestyle will continue for the two of them, as long as their health will allow, which I do hope is far many, many years.

Larry and Dee are two of my favorite people in the whole world and I will always remember when I was best man at their wedding, a wedding which we took to new heights.

Hostage Situation/
Assault in 4ᵗᴴ Degree

April 1, 1993 started out with an early phone call at 5:50 AM from a distraught mother. She told me the police were needed at her daughter's residence, right away. She said her son-in-law, who we'll refer to as Don, had called her and told her he had assaulted her daughter and she needed to come and get her. I asked what else he said and the lady said her daughter's vehicle was coming up her driveway and she had to go. She terminated the conversation without any further comment. (NOTE: *Don was the defendant in an earlier case who came to the Seldovia Police Department and confessed to numerous Fish and Wildlife violations.*)

I was gearing up to respond when the police phone rang a second time. The call was from the same lady and this time she told me her daughter, who will refer to as Sarah, had arrived at her house with her two-year-old grandson. She said her daughter had a bruise and swelling on the side of her face, where Don had struck her. She also told me Don had called a second time and told her he was going to take his kids and go back stateside, to where he was raised. She said the four-year-old girl and both boys, six and seven years of age, were still at the residence with their father. Don also told her, if the police were called, they should be prepared for a fight, because he was loading his weapons and wasn't going to go to jail.

I asked the lady if her daughter needed medical attention and she said she didn't know but, she would check and, if she did, she would take her in to see Doctor Reynolds. The lady then said Sarah requested the EMTs not be called. I asked her if Don was intoxicated and she said Sarah told her he had been drinking. I told Sarah's mother not to go near her daughter's residence and I assured her I would take care of the matter. I told her I would contact her as soon as everyone was safe.

I knew Don very well, and I'd had a number of contacts with him, both police related as well as personal. I was hopeful we had a good enough rapport, wherein I could defuse the situation through a conversation, and not have to call for reinforcements. If he wasn't too intoxicated, it's possible he could be reasoned with. I certainly had nothing to lose by trying, so I dialed his number.

When Don answered the phone, I told him who was calling and he immediately became angry and told me he wasn't going to be taken without a fight. He said he had his guns loaded, and on the table, and he would be ready for me. He went on to say Sarah had been going out to the bars and was drinking and he was sure she was cheating on him. He'd had enough, and said he wasn't going to take it anymore. I stayed quiet on the phone and let him rant and rave. When he was talking about the police intervening, he would yell, but when he was talking about his relationship with his wife, he would cry. Knowing him as I did, I was convinced he was intoxicated and, because of the alcohol involvement, I felt he was very unstable and I didn't know when he might crack. At one point he told me he had been out in the woods yesterday with a shotgun and had actually stuck the barrel into his mouth and was contemplating suicide. I ask him what stopped him and he said he was thinking about his children. He said he didn't care anymore and all he wanted to do was to take his children, go back stateside, where he had been raised, and raise his children away from his wife. I told him the courts would never let him have the kids, in a custody battle, if they knew he held his children hostage and threatened to kill the police when we came to the residence. Don told me he planned to get the children out of the house before any shooting started, but he was not going to go to jail.

I felt very inadequate, trying to negotiate with Don, never having been trained in hostage negotiations, or for that matter, any negotiations. I felt the only thing I could do was use common sense and hope for the best. In that vein, I told Don he had broken the law and I couldn't undo what was already done, but he had to end it here, before something more serious happened and someone was seriously hurt, or even killed. I told him he had to take the responsibility of ending this because he had initiated it. I explained to him, we had to deal with the assault before we could even talk about the custody of the children. Don became angry again and yelled at me saying, "Well then, you've got yourself a fight," and he hung up the phone.

I immediately called Corporal Dan Weatherly of the Alaska State troopers in Homer. I told him about the situation and about Don hanging up on me. I also told him about Don's statement regarding his saying, "You've got yourself a fight." I made the trooper aware Don had assaulted his wife and had loaded his guns and put them on the table. Corporal Weatherly said he would call the Soldotna post of the Alaska State Troopers, and would get back to me and let me know what they decided.

After talking with Corporal Weatherly, I again called Don, in hopes we could come to some arrangement so we would not have to use force to end this. When Don answered, he was more rational and reiterated the problems he and Sarah had been having. He said she was repeatedly coming home drunk, late at night, and she was so intoxicated, she could not remember where she'd been or who she had been with. He said he had been so distraught he'd gone out drinking last night and, because of the alcohol, he had returned home and assaulted his wife. He said, if not for the alcohol, the assault would never have happened. He told me he was a good man and was sorry he had assaulted his wife but he said he was at the end of his rope. I told him, even though he felt he was getting the short end of the stick, we still needed to do something to end this problem without further violence. I told him the way I viewed it, he had two problems, the first being the problem with his marriage and, the second being the fact that he had broken the law. I told him I hoped he and I were good enough friends we could work this out without my having to bring in the Alaska State Troopers. I then told him I had already called the troopers but, I could call them off if he and I could come to an agreement and end this. I assured him we were not going away until this matter was resolved. One way or another, he would be taken into custody for the assault on his wife. If he continued to resist, he could end up separated from his children for a very long time. He had a decision to make, I told him, and that decision could negatively affect the rest of his life, if he made a bad choice. But, I said, the right decision would certainly be taken into consideration by the court.

Don became very apologetic, at this point, and said he knew he had done wrong and he didn't want to hurt anybody, but he just couldn't take any more of this. I told him I had not lied to him and I would continue to be truthful, but he also had to be truthful with me. I explained no one had been seriously injured or killed, at this point, but it had to end here. Don continued to apologize and finally agreed to turn himself in to me at the police department. He said he would drop his kids by his mother-in-law's house and then drive into town. I told him he would be breaking another law, that being DWI. I said he knew he was too intoxicated to be driving a vehicle and I suggested I drive out and pick him up at his residence. I said we could then deliver the children to their grandparent's home on our way into town. Don agreed, and said there would be no more problems. He said he was going to unload all his guns and put them away, as soon as he got off the phone with me. I reminded him, it was very important for him to be totally honest with me and not go back on his word. I told him I would be coming to his residence and he was to follow his three children out of the house with nothing in his hands. I told him I was trusting him, and hopefully, he would be as honest with me as I had been with him. NOTE: *Having dealt with Don numerous times in the past, I knew he placed a lot of emphasis on honesty and, due to this, I was using the honesty angle to negotiate with him.* I reiterated, I would drive up into his driveway and honk the horn, at which time he and his children would come out of the house and get into the police vehicle. I emphasized it was very important that, at all times, he kept his hands visible where I could see them. He said he understood and he would do as directed and be ready to go when I arrived.

After terminating the phone call with Don, I immediately called John Gruber and explained to him what was taking place and asked if he would accompany me. He said he would get geared up and be waiting to be picked up. I then called Corporal Weatherly and told him of the new developments in the case. Corporal Weatherly told me the SART team, AST's Kenai Peninsula SWAT team, were responding out of the Soldotna AST post. He said they were driving down from Soldotna and should be arriving in Homer in approximately forty minutes. Corporal Weatherly said he would contact them and let them know what had developed. He requested I let him know when the suspect was in custody and was no longer a threat. I told him I would notify him, via radio, through Homer police dispatch, as soon as the arrest was made.

I responded to Officer Gruber's residence and picked him up and then drove to Don's residence. Don's residence was located a few miles out of town. Before reaching the driveway, leading up to the house, I stopped and had Officer Gruber get in the back seat directly behind me. We were going to be driving up a driveway, which would leave us vulnerable if, for any reason, Don changed his mind. I explained to Officer Gruber, we would be open targets when we were driving up the driveway. I also wanted him in the back seat so, when we arrived, he could take up a position on the right rear, behind the vehicle, using it for cover. I would be exiting the vehicle and would have the engine block between me and the suspect. It was just a matter of planning for the worst and hoping for the best. I told Officer Gruber to be vigilant and keep his eyes open. I don't think I even needed to voice that though.

As soon as we reached the residence, I honked the horn and both Officer Gruber and I exited the police vehicle and took up our positions. The three children were the first to walk out of the house and down the steps, as was the plan. Don exited the home directly behind his children. He kept his hands out in front of him until he reached the vehicle. I then directed him to place his hands on the side of the vehicle, and I patted him down for weapons. Officer Gruber assisted the three children into the back seat of the vehicle and I told Don to take the front passenger seat. As soon as Don was seated, Officer Gruber took up a position in the rear seat, directly behind him, where he could react if things turned bad. Since everything was going as planned, up to this point, I decided not to place Don in handcuffs in front of the children. I felt they had been through enough trauma this morning, and I didn't want to do anything that would trigger a violent response from Don.

I backed out of the driveway and drove to Don's mother-in-law's home. I then delivered the children to their mother. After the children had exited the vehicle, and were inside the home, I handcuffed Don's hands in front of him. I asked Officer Gruber to watch Don while I contacted Sarah. I observed the swelling and discoloration on the side of Sarah's face and I suggested she contact Doctor Reynolds and get examined. She agreed and said she would. I told her to sign a release of information form so I could get the doctors report for the case.

As we were driving out of the driveway, I called Homer's police dispatch, via radio, and told them to inform Corporal Weatherly I was 1080 and the threat no longer existed. I told them to convey to the trooper we were in route to the Seldovia Police Department. (*1080 is code for having a suspect in custody.*)

Upon reaching the Seldovia police department, Don was booked and was placed in the holding cell. I received a call from Corporal Weatherly and he told me the SART team had been called and had turned around and were on their way back to Soldotna. The Corporal told me, a trooper would be coming to Seldovia on a helicopter, to pick up the suspect and transport him to Homer. He said they would call to give me an estimated time of arrival. Corporal Weatherly further stated they would conduct an interview with the suspect so I wouldn't need to worry about that part of the case.

At approximately 10:20 AM, Bob Larson, pilot of Helo One, *the helicopter owned by the state of Alaska, Department of Public Safety,* landed in Seldovia and Don was turned over to Trooper Carl Schramm and was transported to the Homer jail.

After Don had been turned over to the Alaska State Troopers, and transported to Homer, I called Sarah and asked if she could come to town for an interview. Sarah arrived and was interviewed, on record, at the Seldovia Police Department at approximately 12:02 PM, 4/1/93.

Sarah stated she and Don had been having marital problems for some time now. She said on 3/27/93, Don had taken a shotgun and had gone out into the woods, only to return a short time later. After he returned, she said he told her he was going into town to see the police because he could not take it anymore and he was going crazy. She said he left, only to return a few minutes later. He told her he had gone out into the woods earlier with plans to kill himself but, he realized he was not the problem, she was. She said he then pointed the shotgun at her and said he was going to kill her. She said she was frightened and pulled a blanket over her head. He told her to take the blanket off, because he wanted to look at her when he shot her. She said she refused to take the blanket off, and after a while, he calmed down and put the shotgun away. Sarah said, after he had put the gun away, they tried talking it out and they spent the day together with the children.

She said this morning, being 4/1/93, at approximately 5:30 AM, Don arrived home after drinking all night. When he came home, he started yelling at her about the people she was drinking with on the previous night. In his intoxicated state, he grabbed her and threw her to the floor and started punching her in the side of the head, in the back of the head and on her back. The assault continued for approximately 5 to 10 minutes and, at one point, she said he choked her to the point she nearly passed out. She showed me marks on her neck, which were readily visible, and were consistent with being choked. Sarah said, when the assault finally ended, Don told her he was going to call her mother to come and get her. She said she went into the two-year-old's bedroom and had to change his diaper. She then put her shoes on to take the dirty diaper and put it outside in the garbage on the porch. When she came back in, Don was going to the bedroom, bringing his guns out, and putting them on the table. Sarah said he was also loading them. He told her he was getting ready for when the cops came. When Don had gone to the bedroom for another gun, Sarah said she saw her two-year-old standing near the door and she saw an opportunity, so she grabbed the two-year-old, wrapped him in Don's jacket, and ran out to the vehicle. She said she put the two-year-old in the passenger seat and then ran around to the driver's side, got in the car and backed down the driveway, in an attempt to escape. When she was backing down the driveway, Don ran out on the porch with a rifle, and shot at the right front tire twice, flattening it. She said he could as easily have shot her. Sarah ended her statement by telling me she had gone to the doctor and he had informed her she could have a fractured skull in the area behind her ear. He said there could be other complications as well and they would have to watch her closely. She said she had signed a waiver and the doctor was going to give me the written report. I also encouraged Sarah to get a temporary restraining order, (TRO) and I told her I would help her with the paperwork. She said she would go see the doctor and then come back and we would apply for the order. I thanked her and told her, if she thought of anything else, to let me know, and she left the police department.

Up until the time of the interview, I was not aware any shots had been fired. Following my being told about the shooting, I traveled to Sarah's mother's home and took the tire off the right front of the vehicle. The tire was flat and had two bullet holes through it and the rim. I kept the tire and the rim as evidence. I can honestly say, had I known shots had already been fired, I most probably would have waited for the SART team to arrive. If AST had responded this could have turned out very differently. I guess we will never know for sure but I'm so glad it ended the way it did.

Trooper Schramm called me and asked that I contact Sarah and ascertain if she was ever in fear for her life, at any time when he shot at the vehicle. I contacted Sarah and asked her if she was ever in fear for her life. She stated she thought he was going to shoot at her after she failed to stop, following the tire being shot out. She thought she was going to die, she said. Sarah also told me she was afraid a bullet would hit her two-year-old, since he was sitting in the passenger side, in the front seat of the vehicle. I asked her if she was in fear for her life when he threatened her with a shotgun when she had the blanket over her head. She said she was in fear when he was choking her and at one point, she thought she might die.

At approximately 3:25 PM, on the same day, I interviewed Sarah's mother while we were sitting in the police vehicle outside of her residence. She said Don had called her early this morning and told her to come and get her daughter, and said he was fed up with her going out and drinking and he was going to take the kids and leave. She said after he hung up, she started getting dressed and the phone rang again. Don called her a second time and told her to hurry up and come and get her daughter. He said he had beat her up. Sarah's mother said she told Don, if he touched her daughter again, she would call the police. Don told her to go ahead, because he was loading his guns and, when the police showed up, someone was going to get killed. She said she immediately called me, following his call, and reported what he told her. She said she had to hang up when she saw her daughter driving up the driveway. She observed bruising and swelling on the left side of her daughter's face. She said, after her daughter had arrived at her house, Don had called again. This time he told her he was taking the children and leaving for the states. He said he would not leave the kids with their mother because she didn't take care of them. Sarah's mother ended her statement by saying she did not know anything about him shooting at the tire until after I had arrested Don.

Following the interview, I traveled to Sarah and Don's residence and met with Sarah. I told her I wanted to get photographs of Sarah's injuries, as well as the home and its contents, including all the weapons that were in the home. I wound up confiscating seven weapons, made up of shotguns and rifles, and I took into evidence all the ammunition we could find for the weapons. Those, along with the tire and rim of the vehicle, were logged into evidence and locked in the evidence room at the Seldovia Police Department.

Numerous charges were brought against Don by the Alaska State Troopers. He was charged with assault in the 3rd degree for threatening to shoot his wife with the shotgun on 3/27/93. He was charged with assault in the 4th degree for striking his wife in the face, head and in the back and he was charged with a second charge of assault in the 3rd degree for shooting at the vehicle when Sarah was backing down the driveway. Don was also charged with reckless endangerment, because when he shot at the vehicle his two-year-old son was sitting on the passenger side, and was recklessly endangered by Don's actions. The Alaska State Troopers also charged him with misconduct involving weapons in the 2nd degree for being in possession of a firearm while he was intoxicated. Because there were two felonies charged, the court would not accept a plea without first appointing an attorney for Don. After an attorney was appointed, Don pled not guilty and a trial date was set. Bail was set at $5000, cash only, and because Don couldn't make bail, he was held in jail.

A disposition was finally reached, after Don changed his plea to no contest on charges of assault in the 3rd degree and assault in the 4tho degree. The other charges were dismissed per a plea agreement between the district attorney and Don's court appointed attorney. On the charges of assault in the 3rd degree and assault in the 4th degree, Don was sentenced to 365 days in jail with 195 days suspended and he was placed on probation for five years. Don was also ordered to report for alcohol screening and in-house treatment for ninety days. It was also ordered, if it was deemed necessary through the alcohol screening process, he was to undergo a mental evaluation. He was to have no criminal offenses within his probation timeframe and he was ordered to keep in contact with his probation officer on a monthly basis. He was given credit for the time he had already spent in jail and for any good time he had accumulated.

Don had been served the temporary restraining order and could not go back to his home without court permission, after he was released from jail. Don completed his alcohol screening and his in-house treatment and he and Sarah were divorced following his release. (Case closed by arrest)

NOTE: *It is not a common occurrence for a hostage situation, such as this, to occur in the smaller communities. However, we had to always be ready to respond to any call for assistance on the side of the Bay. Even though the Alaska State Troopers are responsible for any crimes committed outside our city limits, we responded on their behalf. The City of Seldovia held a contract with the Department of Public Safety, agreeing to respond to any*

AST calls for assistance in state jurisdiction. The officers of the Seldovia Police Department held AST commissions, which gave us AST powers outside the city limits, and throughout the State of Alaska. The contract came into being in 1981, after I had attended the Alaska State Trooper academy in Sitka, Alaska. Had we not been able to convince Don to give himself up, AST would have flown to Seldovia and would have taken over the police response. I am very glad Don decided to come out, under his own power. This again proves it is not only the larger, more populated, communities where serious felony crimes occur, and even in small communities, life-and-death situations have to be addressed.

DWI/Refuse Breath Test]

In 1993, Kevin Stevenson joined the Seldovia police force as a patrol officer. Kevin had not been a police officer prior to joining the Seldovia Police Department, but he had, at his own expense, put himself through the Alaska State Trooper police academy in Sitka, Alaska. Kevin had worked as a security guard in southeast Alaska but told me his lifelong dream was to be a sworn police officer. I could see a lot of potential and drive in him, so he was the man chosen for the position, out of a number of applicants. When Kevin joined the force, he moved his wife, Jessica, and their three children, to Seldovia. Jessica became a very valued member of our local EMT squad. Both she and Kevin were great assets to Seldovia, while they were here. Kevin stayed with me for three years, before moving back to southeastern Alaska. In Craig he took the position as a police officer and stayed there for a number of years before moving to Anchorage and joining the University of Alaska Police Department. Kevin is still with the University Police Department. I still stay in touch with him and the family as much as possible. His children are now grown, with families of their own and everyone seems to be doing well.

Officer Stevenson worked nights and I covered days, in our department. On the night of July 25, 1993, at approximately 3:06 AM, Officer Stevenson observed a vehicle, a gray and black Ford pickup truck, traveling westerly on Main Street. He observed the vehicle swerve abruptly to the right, into the parking lot at the Centurion Restaurant. The vehicle then swerved back onto the roadway and across the centerline and continued in a westerly direction. The vehicle then attempted to turn right on Harborview Drive, but stopped in the middle of the turn. The vehicle was then observed to make an abrupt left turn, back onto Main Street and continue in a westerly direction. At Lipke Lane the driver attempted to turn right, and in doing so, hit a log, which was on the side of the roadway. He then backed away from the log, and made an abrupt left turn into the parking lot at the clinic, where he brought the vehicle to a stop. Officer Stevenson, C4, pulled up behind the pickup with his overhead lights activated on his patrol vehicle. The officer then made contact with the driver and recognized the man, who we will refer to as Jesse. A passenger, who was not known by the officer, was also observed to be in the vehicle.

C4 asked Jesse where he was headed and Jesse told the officer he was just driving around town. C4 immediately observed Jesse's slurred speech and further observed his bloodshot, and watery eyes. The officer asked Jesse to exit the vehicle and, upon doing so, he observed Jesse to be very unstable on his feet, staggering and using the vehicle for support so he would not fall. At this point C4 called me on the radio and told me he had made a vehicle stop and would, most probably, be needing me for a breath test. C4 was not certified on the Intoximeter, so I had to respond at any time there was an arrest for DWI, to administer the test.

The officer told Jesse he would be putting him through some field sobriety test to ascertain his degree of intoxication. Surprisingly, Jesse was compliant and attempted the tests.

The first test was the horizontal gaze nystagmus test. The test is made up of three parts. While the officer observed the eyes of the subject, he moves an object, some sort of stimulus, from left to right, which the subject follows with his eyes only, without moving his head. The officer checks for a smooth pursuit of the eyes, how the eyes react, when held at a maximum deviation, and how the eyes react at a 45-degree angle. In administering this test, the officer found the subject failed all three tests. When alcohol is in the system, the eyes will jerk somewhat, when moving left to right, and vice versa. When the eye is held at maximum deviation, whether to the left or to the right, excessive alcohol on board will cause the eye to jerk. The onset of the jerking motion of the eye, is an indication of how much alcohol has been consumed. If the eye started a jerking movement at, or before, it is in a 45-degree angle, the officer can assume the driver is impaired. However, more tests are given so you are not limiting yourself to only the horizontal gaze nystagmus test, to determine if there is enough probable cause for an arrest for DWI. During the test, Jesse had difficulty in taking direction, and in focusing on the pen the officer was using for the stimulus.

C4 then asked Jesse to recite the American alphabet, from the letter "A" to the letter "Z." Jesse attempted this on two occasions but each time he was unable to complete the test. C4 then directed Jesse to count backwards, from 100 to 50 by 5's. The officer had to repeat his request a second time and, even though he demonstrated the test, when Jesse attempted it, he counted forward, from 50 to 100, by 5's, instead of counting backwards. Jesse even failed to complete that correctly. Jesse was then directed to stand with his arms at his sides, and to lift one leg approximately 6 inches off the ground, then to count to thirty, while staying in that position. He was directed to count using one 1000, two 1000, three 1000, etc. Jesse did not even attempt this test and told the officer he could not do the test, because he was too drunk. (*An officer always loves hearing this type response when testing for probable cause to arrest for DWI.*) The last test the officer directed Jesse to do was the heel to toe test. Jesse was told to walk eight steps forward, to turn and takes six steps back, touching his toe on one foot with the heel of the opposite foot, on each step. Jesse walked up approximately five steps, turned around and walked back to the officer. Not one time did he touch his toe with the heel of his opposite foot. He also staggered when he was attempting the test.

At this point C4 told Jesse he was under arrest for DWI and he placed him in handcuffs. Following the arrest, C4 patted Jesse down for weapons, and then placed him in the patrol vehicle. The officer then contacted the passenger in the vehicle to ascertain his degree of intoxication. Jesse wanted the vehicle turned over to the passenger, but the officer had to ensure the passenger was not impaired, and was a licensed driver, before he could turn the vehicle over to him. Upon contacting the passenger, the officer found him to be sober and to have a valid operator's license. C4 informed the man, Jesse had been arrested for DWI and Jesse requested the vehicle be turned over to him. The officer told him he was free to go.

C4, upon returning to his vehicle, was going to administer a portable breath test, (PBT), but Jesse had passed out while setting in the warm vehicle. After attempting to wake him, and being unsuccessful, C4 decided to transport him to the police department where I could administer the Intoximeter breath test. C4 transported Jesse to the police department and was able to wake him up, after a time, and walked him inside.

I had arrived at the Seldovia Police Department just prior to C4 bringing Jesse in and I had activated the voice tape recorder to record any statements and to record the booking procedure. Jesse was upset and argumentative when they arrived at the police department. Jesse was well aware of what was about to take place because he was a frequent flyer, he was one of those I referred to as job security. I knew as long as Jesse was in town, I would have a job. It seemed Jesse could not stay out of trouble. He drank heavily and, anytime he was intoxicated, it seemed, we became involved.

I read the Miranda rights warning to Jesse and gave him an opportunity to tell me his side of the story, but he refused to sign the waiver and told me he wasn't doing anything without first talking to his attorney. I ask him for his attorney's phone number, and told him I would call him. He said he didn't have the number and I gave him a phonebook. Jesse was unable to come up with the number for his attorney, so I told him he had to decide for himself whether he wanted to talk to me or not.

After observing him for approximately twenty-five minutes, I asked Jesse to provide me with a sample of his breath. Again, Jesse told me he was not going to do anything until he talked to his attorney. I tried to reason with him, telling him we needed a phone number for his attorney, so he could be reached. After a time, and after more heated conversation on his part, Jesse finally agreed to give me a breath sample.

I set up the Intoximeter and Jesse blew only slightly into the mouth-piece, and the Intoximeter aborted the test. This wasn't my first rodeo and I knew he was just jacking me around, but I gave him two more opportunities to give me a good breath sample. The last time I gave him an opportunity to blow, I told him, if he chose to keep screwing around, and didn't give me an adequate breath sample, I would charge him with refusal to give a breath sample, and I then read him the implied consent warning. On the third attempt, he again blew only slightly into the mouthpiece, and again the Intoximeter aborted the test. It was at that time I charged him with refusal to give a breath sample, another class A misdemeanor.

After he was charged with refusal to blow, we put him through the booking procedure, where he was fingerprinted and photographed and then placed in the jail cell. All during this time Jesse was argumentative and insulting to both myself and C4. We found this to be normal for Jesse, when he was intoxicated.

Jesse was held until 1:00 PM, 7/25/93, at which time he was released on his own recognizance after signing a promise to appear for arraignment on 7/29/93, at 1:30 PM, and agreeing to abstain from any alcohol consumption until that time.

At arraignment Jesse pled guilty to DWI, and the refusal to give a breath sample was dismissed. Jesse had contacted his attorney, following his release from the Seldovia jail, and his attorney and the district attorney had reached an agreement to drop the second charge, if Jesse agreed to plead guilty to DWI. Since Jesse was a repeat offender, with a previous DWI, his sentence was considerably more than a first-time offender. He was given a $1000 fine with $500 suspended; he was ordered to serve 120 days in jail with 100 days suspended, and he was ordered to report to Homer jail within two days. His operator's license was revoked for one year and he was ordered to surrender it immediately to the court. He was further ordered to undertake alcohol screening at SKIAP, our local alcoholism program. He was ordered to report to SKIAP, as soon as he was released from jail. He was also ordered to pay any costs for the program but, the judge told him, the cost could be applied toward is fine. Jesse was placed on probation for two years, with conditions he comply with the alcohol screening, and pay all fees, and he was not to commit any criminal acts within his probationary period. (Case Closed by Arrest)

NOTE: *I do hope you have enjoyed reading about all the police related happenings in, and around, Seldovia in this book, as well as my first publication. This finishes the second book, in a four-book series, of Alaska Bush Cop. Hopefully, I can have another book ready for publishing in the spring of 2021.*

If you enjoyed the read, tell your friends and neighbors about my books. If you, or your friends, are interested in poetry, or stories in rhyme, you might want to check out my first book, *Ramblings of an Alaskan Bush Poet*. My second book, *Before the Badge*, contains seven short stories of the exciting life I lived, at times life-threatening, from the time I reached Alaska, in 1964 until 1979, when I was sworn in as the chief of police for the city of Seldovia.

You can check out my website at www.andyandersonbooks.com or you can email me at andynann6@gmail.com, if you're interested in obtaining any of my work. I also can be found on Facebook under *A. W. Anderson*. I hope to be hearing from you so, until next time, stay healthy and God bless.

www.ingramcontent.com/pod-product-compliance
Lightning Source LLC
Chambersburg PA
CBHW052037090426

42739CB00010B/1950